Charles Darwin's
On the Origin of Species

A graphic adaptation

Story by Michael Keller

Art by Nicolle Rager Fuller

RODALE

Rodale books may be purchased for business or promotional use or for special sales. For information, please write to:
    Special Markets Department
    Rodale Inc.
    733 Third Avenue
    New York, NY 10017

Printed in the United States of America
Rodale Inc. makes every effort to use acid-free ∞, recycled paper ♻.

Book design and illustrations by Nicolle Rager Fuller
Edited by Colin Dickerman

Library of Congress Cataloging-in-Publication Data

Keller, Michael
    Charles Darwin's On the Origin of Species : a graphic adaptation / story by Michael Keller ; art by Nicolle Rager Fuller.
       p.   cm.
    ISBN-10: 1-60529-697-X Hardcover
    ISBN-13: 978-1-60529-697-5 Hardcover
    ISBN-13: 978-1-60529-948-8 Paperback
    ISBN-10: 1-60529-948-0 Paperback
    1. Evolution (Biology)—Comic books, strips, etc. 2. Natural selection—Comic books, strips, etc. 3. Darwin, Charles, 1809-1882. Origin of species—Illustrations. I. Fuller, Nicolle Rager II. Darwin, Charles, 1809-1882. Origin of species. III. Title.
    QH367.K466 2009
    576.8'2—dc22
                                   2009011387

Distributed to the trade by Macmillan

2 4 6 8 10 9 7 5 3 1 Hardcover
2 4 6 8 10 9 7 5 3 1 Paperback

RODALE
LIVE YOUR WHOLE LIFE™

We inspire and enable people to improve their lives and the world around them
For more of our products visit **rodalestore.com** or call 800-848-4735

Contents

Part 1

Beginnings of a Theory

...2 October 1836, Falmouth, England

Ahh, England. After all the years of exploring alien lands across this wide world, tamping underfoot the moist soil of home is a welcome respite.

It feels as though the world left us behind these many years we've been gone. What do you say, Covington?

Aye, it's been a long trip, Mr. Darwin, but a productive one. It's been my honor to assist you with your collection.

Never, I'm sure, has a queen's ship ever been so successful in reconnoitering the shores of a distant coast or its natural history.

I'd say your work has only just begun with all the specimens you've brought back, sir.

You've been a great help these nearly five years.

Driver, to Shrewsbury. I shan't tarry another moment while home awaits.

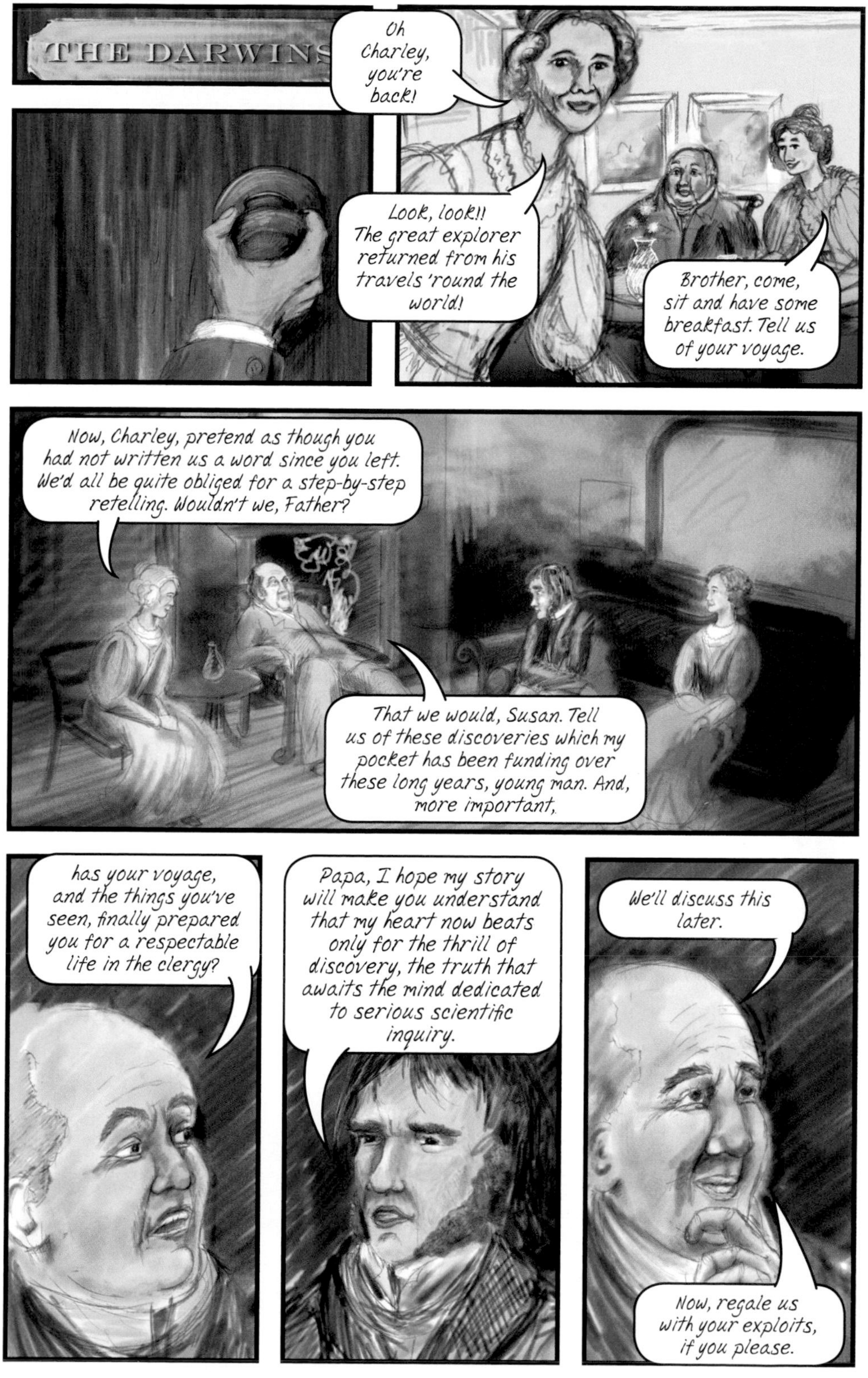
THE DARWINS
Oh Charley, you're back!
Look, look!! The great explorer returned from his travels 'round the world!
Brother, come, sit and have some breakfast. Tell us of your voyage.
Now, Charley, pretend as though you had not written us a word since you left. We'd all be quite obliged for a step-by-step retelling. Wouldn't we, Father?
That we would, Susan. Tell us of these discoveries which my pocket has been funding over these long years, young man. And, more important,
has your voyage, and the things you've seen, finally prepared you for a respectable life in the clergy?
Papa, I hope my story will make you understand that my heart now beats only for the thrill of discovery, the truth that awaits the mind dedicated to serious scientific inquiry.
We'll discuss this later.
Now, regale us with your exploits, if you please.

After having been twice driven back by heavy south-western gales, Her Majesty's ship Beagle, a 10-gun brig, under the command of Captain FitzRoy, sailed from Devonport on the 27th of December 1831. The object of the expedition was to complete the survey of Patagonia and Tierra del Fuego, commenced under Captain King's [earlier four-year mission] to survey the shores of Chile, Peru, and of some islands in the Pacific—and to carry a chain of chronometrical measurements round the World.

GALÁPAGOS— STUDYING ATOLLS AND GEOLOGY

OCTOBER 1835

GALÁPAGOS—COLLECTING SPECIMENS

DEVONPORT

GALÁPAGOS

PATAGONIA

TIERRA DEL FUEGO

RIDING WITH GAUCHOS AFTER RHEAS

MARCH 1835

JULY 1834

It had now been two and a half years on these infernal seas with no end in sight to this expedition. What would become of me hereafter, I knew not; I felt like a ruined man, who did not see or care how to extricate himself. That this voyage would come to a conclusion, my reason told me, but otherwise I saw no end to it.

8

DEVONPORT

DECEMBER 27, 1831

CUTTLEFISH OFF THE COAST OF AFRICA

JANUARY 1832

MARCH 1832

ON DECK READING LYELL'S PRINCIPLES OF GEOLOGY

SEPTEMBER 1832

A FOSSILIZED TOOTH

SEPTEMBER 1832

FUEGIANS

DECEMBER 1832

PACKING UP SPECIMENS, INCLUDING A SCELIDOTHERIUM SKULL

AUGUST 1833

The more I saw, the greater connection I saw between things. From savages in Tierra del Fuego to slave traders up the coast. From the great ostrich in Africa to its smaller cousins the rhea and emu in South America. And, oh, the fossil lines of beach and shell suspended in cliff faces were undoubtedly close to the active shorelines below.

9

The voyage of the Beagle has been by far the most important event in my life and has determined my whole career.

There I am, 22 years old. I had just graduated from Cambridge University and I was selected for the voyage mainly because of a matured interest in studying the natural world.

I was only invited along to be Captain FitzRoy's gentleman companion, not as the expedition naturalist.

Charles Darwin
Born: 12 February 1809
Hometown: Shrewsbury, a market town near the Welsh border
Education: Shrewsbury School. Apprentice doctor for his father. University of Edinburgh to study medicine. Cambridge University
Hobbies: Bird hunting, shooting, reading, insect collecting, geology, horseback riding, partaking in a food challenge club where the participants ate wildlife not normally considered food, writing letters.

Soon enough, I claimed that title for myself. And, oh! how I had been won over by the beauty of the tropics—the insects, plants, volcanoes. It was something I had read about and wished to see for years.

Nobody but a person fond of natural history can imagine the pleasure of strolling under cocoa nuts in a thicket of bananas & coffee plants, and an endless number of wild flowers.

It is utterly useless to say anything about the scenery—

it would be as profitable to explain to a blind man colours, as to a person who has not been out of Europe the total dissimilarity of a tropical view.

Charley, dinner!

Of course, I was not yet a master naturalist. In fact, besides several university classes covering the various disciplines making up natural history, my experience comprised mainly an unrefined interest in the richness of nature.

I could not have imagined the sheer number of discoveries I would collect and send back to England for classification by my group of volunteer scientists. One of those scientists was naturalist Leonard Jenyns, whose seat I was lucky enough to take on the Beagle voyage after Jenyns declined.

I am heartily thankful to Jenyns for having undertaken & gone so thoroughly to work on the fish part of my collection.... I am astonished & glad to hear how many new things he seemed to have found—four new genera is something.

I collected over 3,900 shells, plants, insects, birds, and animals and took copious notes on local geological conditions throughout the voyage. I was much struck with certain facts in the distribution of the organic beings inhabiting South America, and in the geological relations of the present to the past inhabitants of that continent.

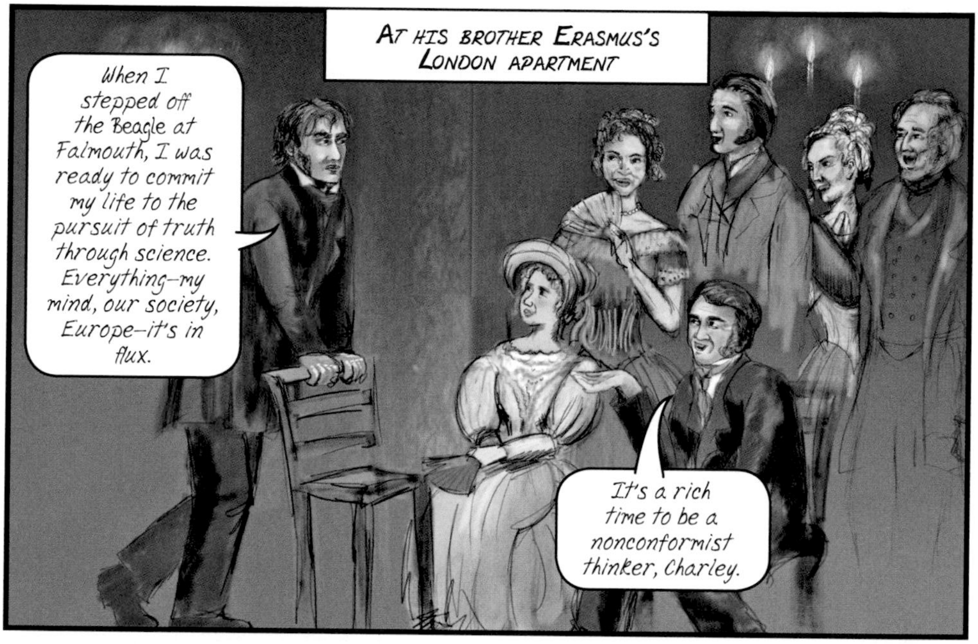
At his brother Erasmus's London apartment
When I stepped off the Beagle at Falmouth, I was ready to commit my life to the pursuit of truth through science. Everything—my mind, our society, Europe—it's in flux.
It's a rich time to be a nonconformist thinker, Charley.

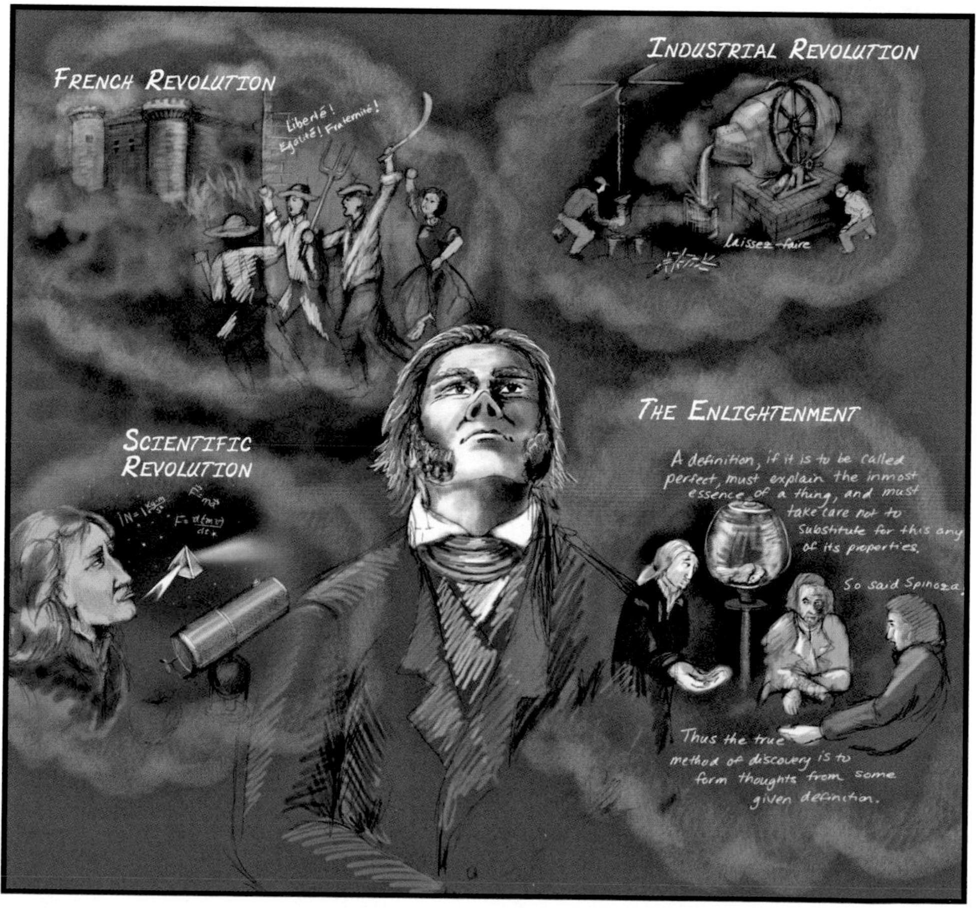
French Revolution
Liberté! Egalité! Fraternité!
Industrial Revolution
laissez-faire
Scientific Revolution
The Enlightenment
A definition, if it is to be called perfect, must explain the inmost essence of a thing, and must take care not to substitute for this any of its properties.
So said Spinoza.
Thus the true method of discovery is to form thoughts from some given definition.

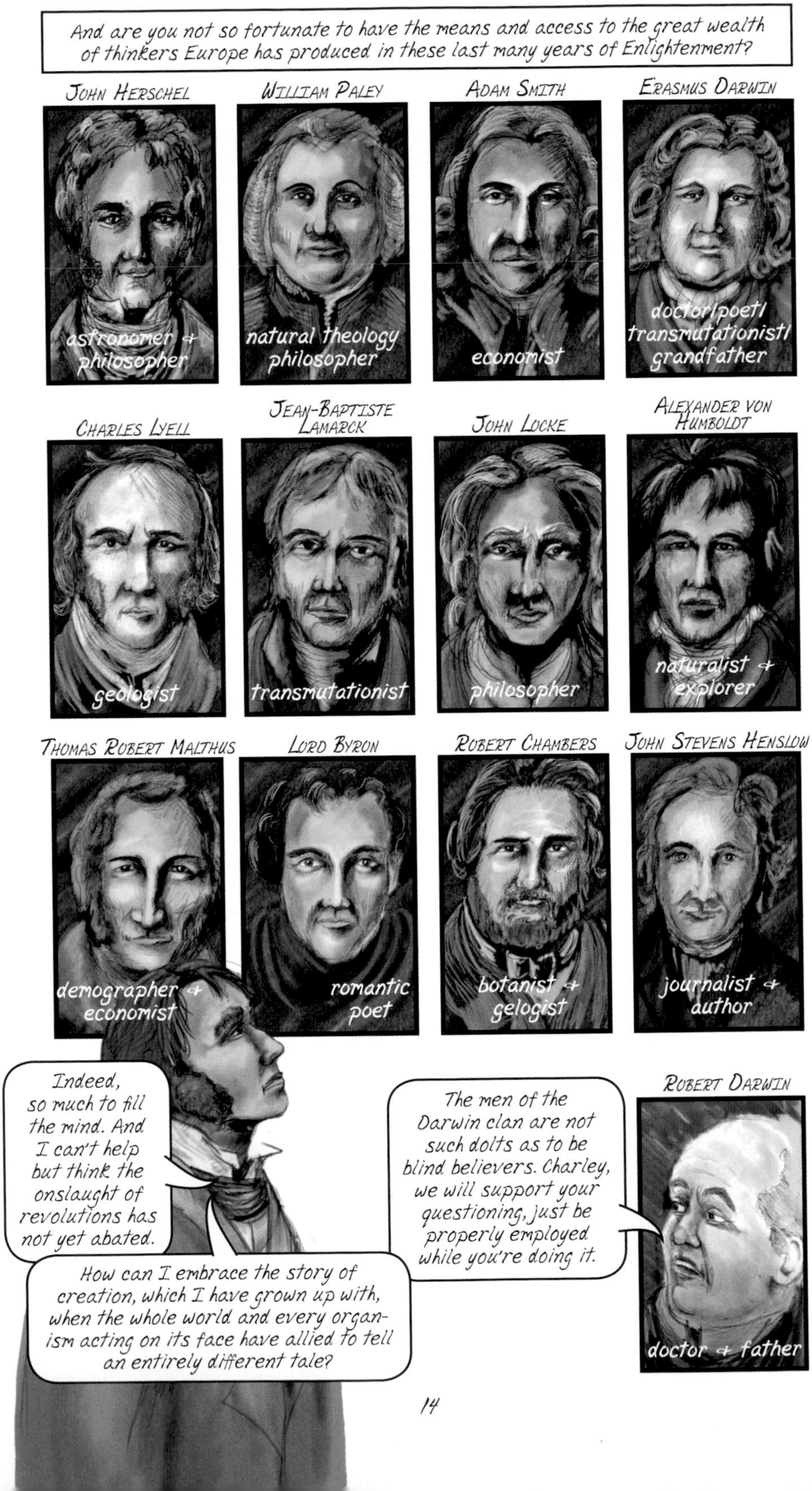

And are you not so fortunate to have the means and access to the great wealth of thinkers Europe has produced in these last many years of Enlightenment?
JOHN HERSCHEL
astronomer + philosopher
WILLIAM PALEY
natural theology philosopher
ADAM SMITH
economist
ERASMUS DARWIN
doctor/poet/ transmutationist/ grandfather
CHARLES LYELL
geologist
JEAN-BAPTISTE LAMARCK
transmutationist
JOHN LOCKE
philosopher
ALEXANDER VON HUMBOLDT
naturalist + explorer
THOMAS ROBERT MALTHUS
demographer + economist
LORD BYRON
romantic poet
ROBERT CHAMBERS
botanist + gelogist
JOHN STEVENS HENSLOW
journalist + author
Indeed, so much to fill the mind. And I can't help but think the onslaught of revolutions has not yet abated.
How can I embrace the story of creation, which I have grown up with, when the whole world and every organism acting on its face have allied to tell an entirely different tale?
ROBERT DARWIN
The men of the Darwin clan are not such dolts as to be blind believers. Charley, we will support your questioning, just be properly employed while you're doing it.
doctor + father

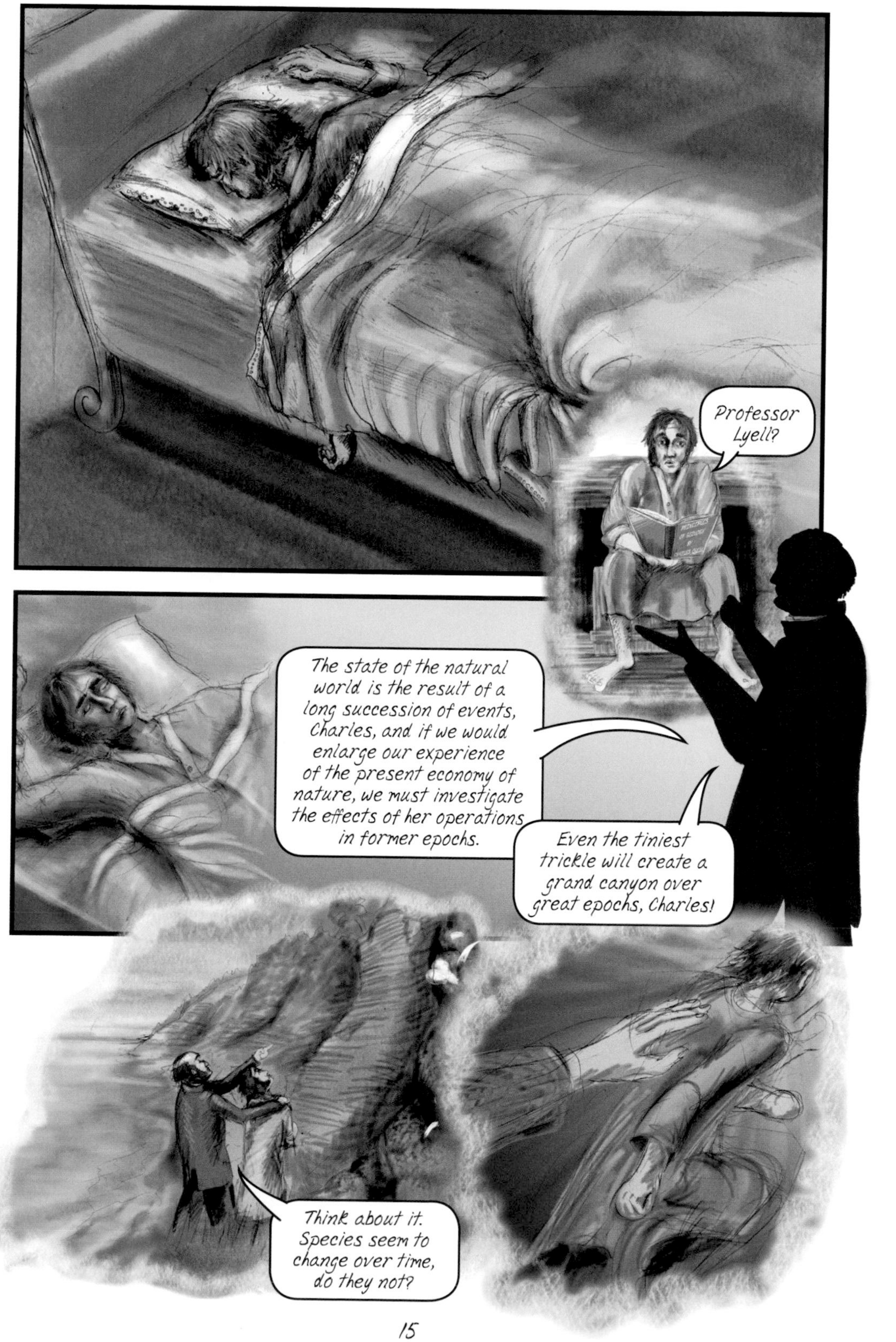
Professor Lyell?
The state of the natural world is the result of a long succession of events, Charles, and if we would enlarge our experience of the present economy of nature, we must investigate the effects of her operations in former epochs.
Even the tiniest trickle will create a grand canyon over great epochs, Charles!
Think about it. Species seem to change over time, do they not?

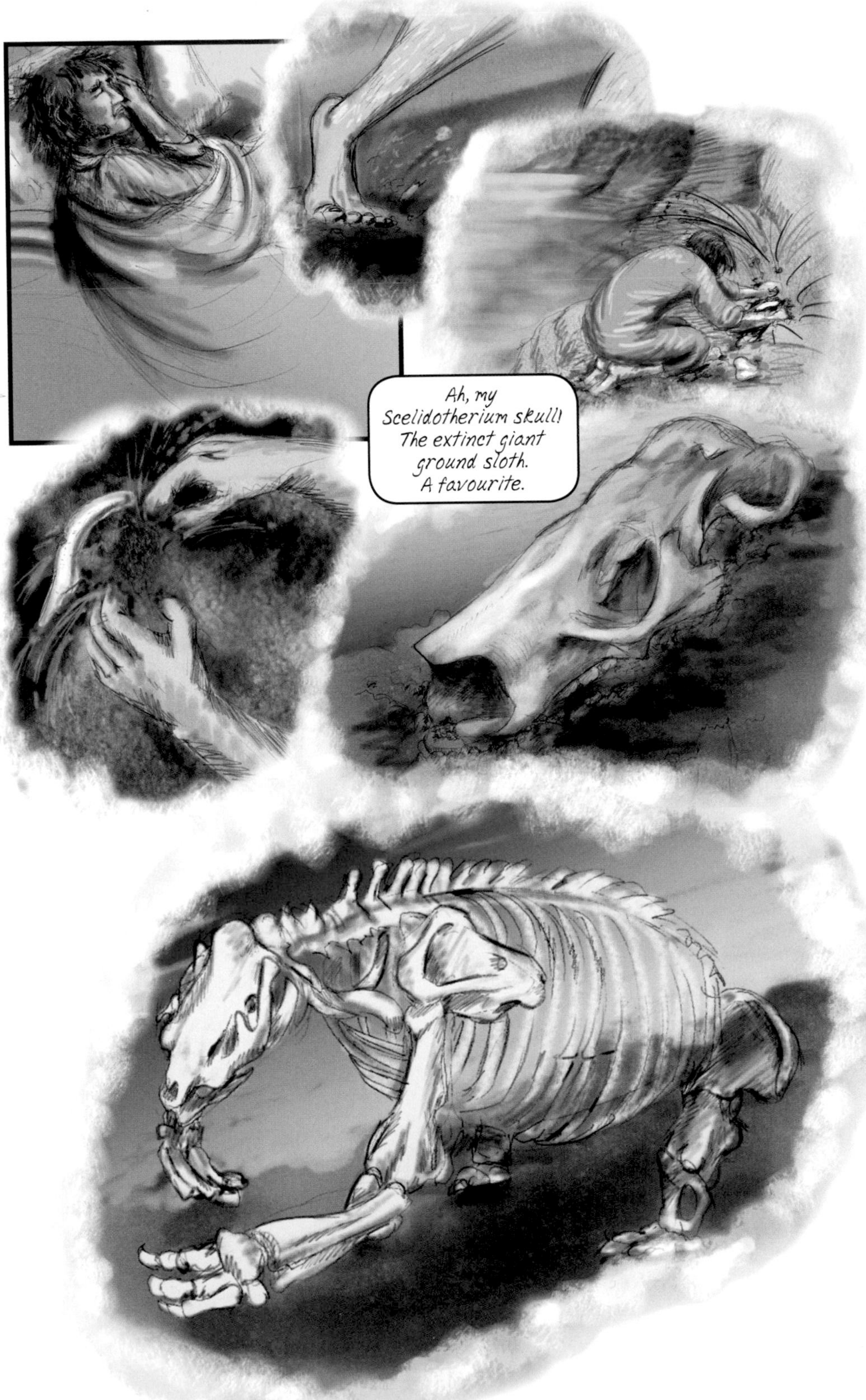
Ah, my Scelidotherium skull! The extinct giant ground sloth. A favourite.

AHHH!

The modern tree sloth. The connection between the extinct animal and the modern one is uncanny.

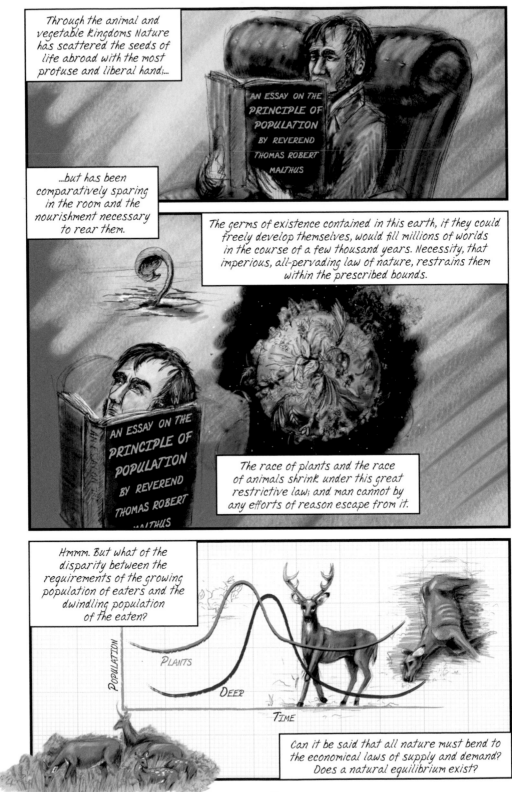

Through the animal and vegetable kingdoms Nature has scattered the seeds of life abroad with the most profuse and liberal hand;...

AN ESSAY ON THE *PRINCIPLE OF POPULATION* BY REVEREND THOMAS ROBERT MALTHUS

...but has been comparatively sparing in the room and the nourishment necessary to rear them.

The germs of existence contained in this earth, if they could freely develop themselves, would fill millions of worlds in the course of a few thousand years. Necessity, that imperious, all-pervading law of nature, restrains them within the prescribed bounds.

AN ESSAY ON THE *PRINCIPLE OF POPULATION* BY REVEREND THOMAS ROBERT MALTHUS

The race of plants and the race of animals shrink under this great restrictive law; and man cannot by any efforts of reason escape from it.

Hmmm. But what of the disparity between the requirements of the growing population of eaters and the dwindling population of the eaten?

POPULATION

PLANTS

DEER

TIME

Can it be said that all nature must bend to the economical laws of supply and demand? Does a natural equilibrium exist?

18

Perhaps limited resources—food, space, water, mates, or other things—are the things that bring individual organisms into conflict. Want of limited things may be one of the very forces changing species over time.

Life is like the inorganic material comprising the Earth, which has been changing over millennia. And the pressures placed on organisms by natural forces, combined with competition between each other, is the mechanism whereby all creatures diverge over time!

PERMANENCE OF SPECIES

Those long years at sea gave me more than boxes of specimens. I find my mind holding the logical key to descent with modification of species as spurred on by the working of a passive natural selection. The hand of God recedes.

DESCENT WITH MODIFICATION

This is something entirely different. I must have facts to support this view.

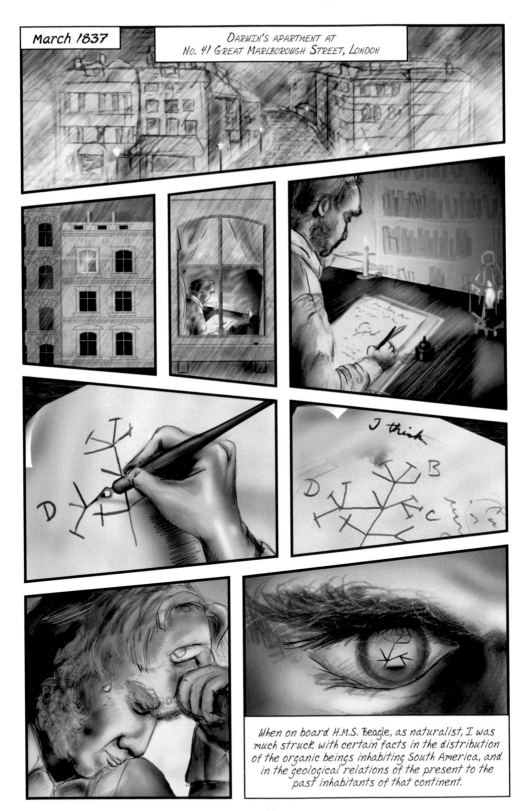

March 1837

DARWIN'S APARTMENT AT
NO. 41 GREAT MARLBOROUGH STREET, LONDON

I think

When on board H.M.S. Beagle, as naturalist, I was
much struck with certain facts in the distribution
of the organic beings inhabiting South America, and
in the geological relations of the present to the
past inhabitants of that continent.

To my imagination it is far more satisfactory to look at such instincts as the young cuckoo ejecting its foster-brothers,

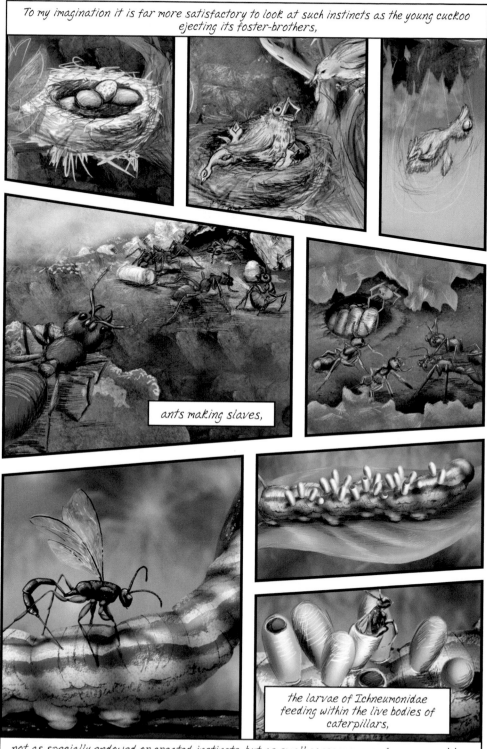

ants making slaves,

the larvae of Ichneumonidae feeding within the live bodies of caterpillars,

not as specially endowed or created instincts, but as small consequences of one general law leading to the advancement of all organic beings, namely,

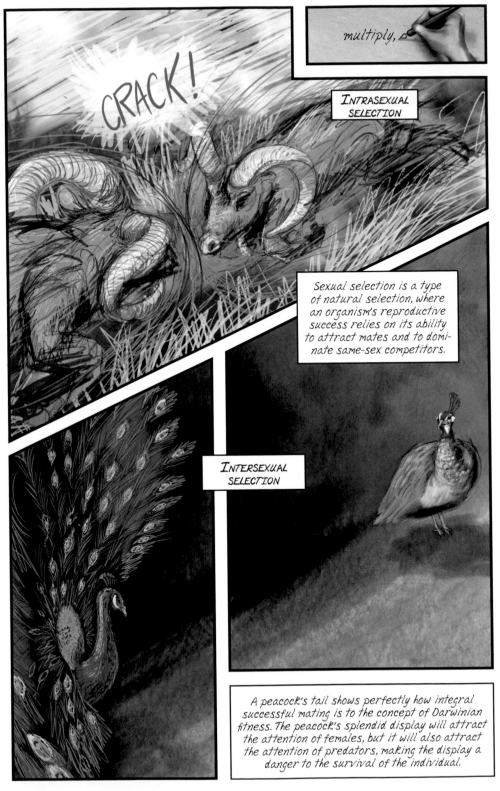

multiply,

CRACK!

Sexual selection is a type of natural selection, where an organism's reproductive success relies on its ability to attract mates and to dominate same-sex competitors.

INTERSEXUAL SELECTION

A peacock's tail shows perfectly how integral successful mating is to the concept of Darwinian fitness. The peacock's splendid display will attract the attention of females, but it will also attract the attention of predators, making the display a danger to the survival of the individual.

vary,

The giraffe, by its lofty stature, much elongated neck, fore-legs, head, and tongue, has its whole frame beautifully adapted for browsing on the higher branches of trees. It can thus obtain food beyond the reach of the other Ungulata or hoofed animals inhabiting the same country, and this must be a great advantage to it during dearths.

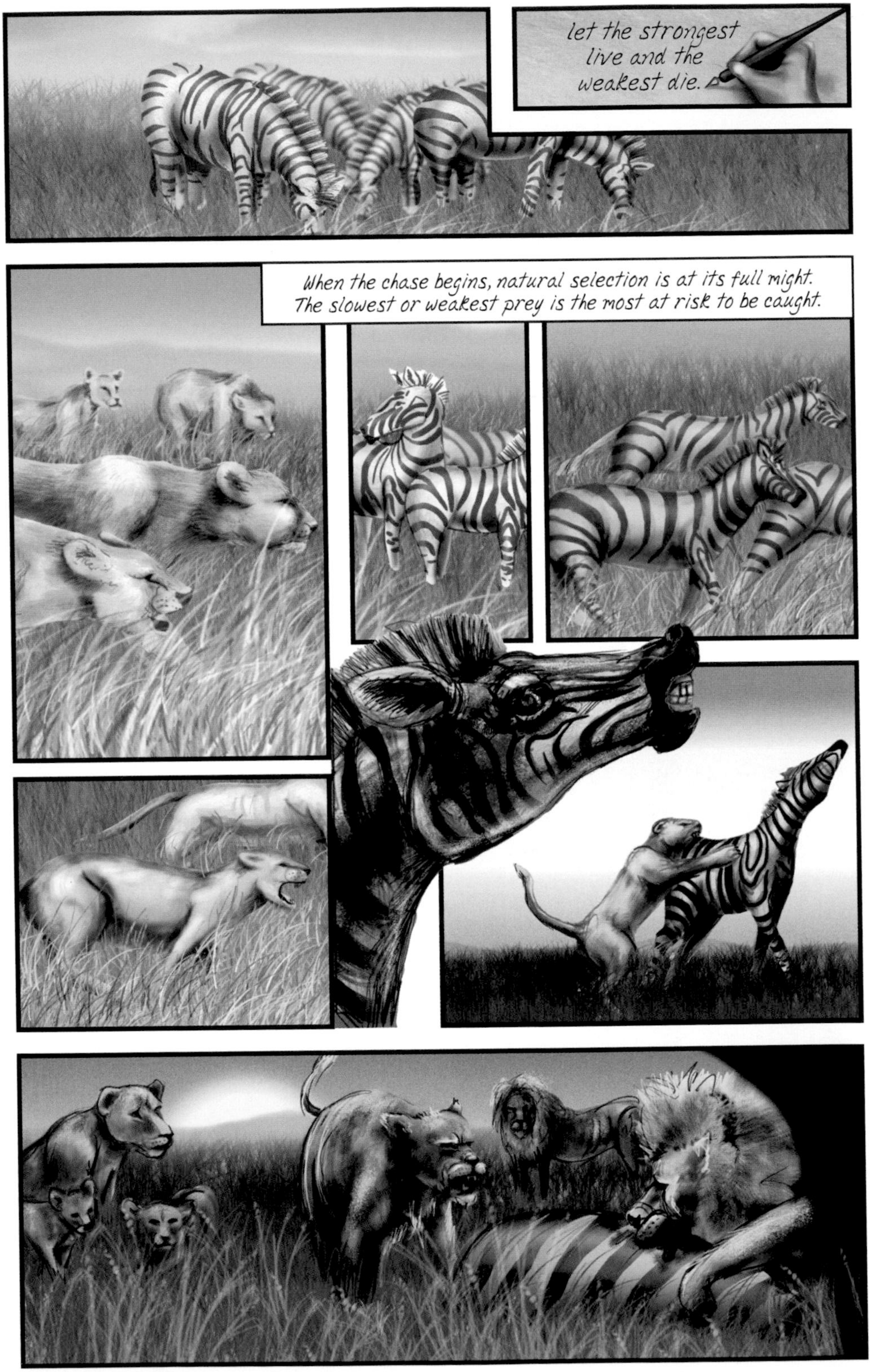
let the strongest live and the weakest die.
When the chase begins, natural selection is at its full might. The slowest or weakest prey is the most at risk to be caught.

I need the expertise of savants throughout the country on many different aspects of breeding crops and animals.

These are important questions which only men like you can answer.

This one's father is a champion stud I've imported from America to strengthen the bloodline.

This greyhound's stock comes from the fastest in all of England. I've got one-up on the other breeders, as well.

My dear Sir,

Will you excuse me troubling you with some questions, which I am very anxious to get answered, and do not know what work to refer to.

How far north do woods of any extent occur? Did I understand you to say that forest trees grew over ground, which at the depth of a few feet was perpetually frozen? I suppose this as much as to say that there may exist extensive woods, where the mean annual temperature is below the freezing point. What trees grow in such cold climates, & do they attain any size? Do plains covered with bushes, occur in any part of the extreme north?

My object in these questions, is to be enabled to compare the mere quantity of vegetation, in parts of South America, where large animals formerly did live, and likewise in Africa where large animals are now living, with the quantity growing in climates far north, and extremely cold. If you would have the kindness to answer me briefly these questions, I should be greatly obliged, but I really ought to apologise for asking you to take so much trouble.... Believe me dear Sir,

Yours most truly, Chas. Darwin

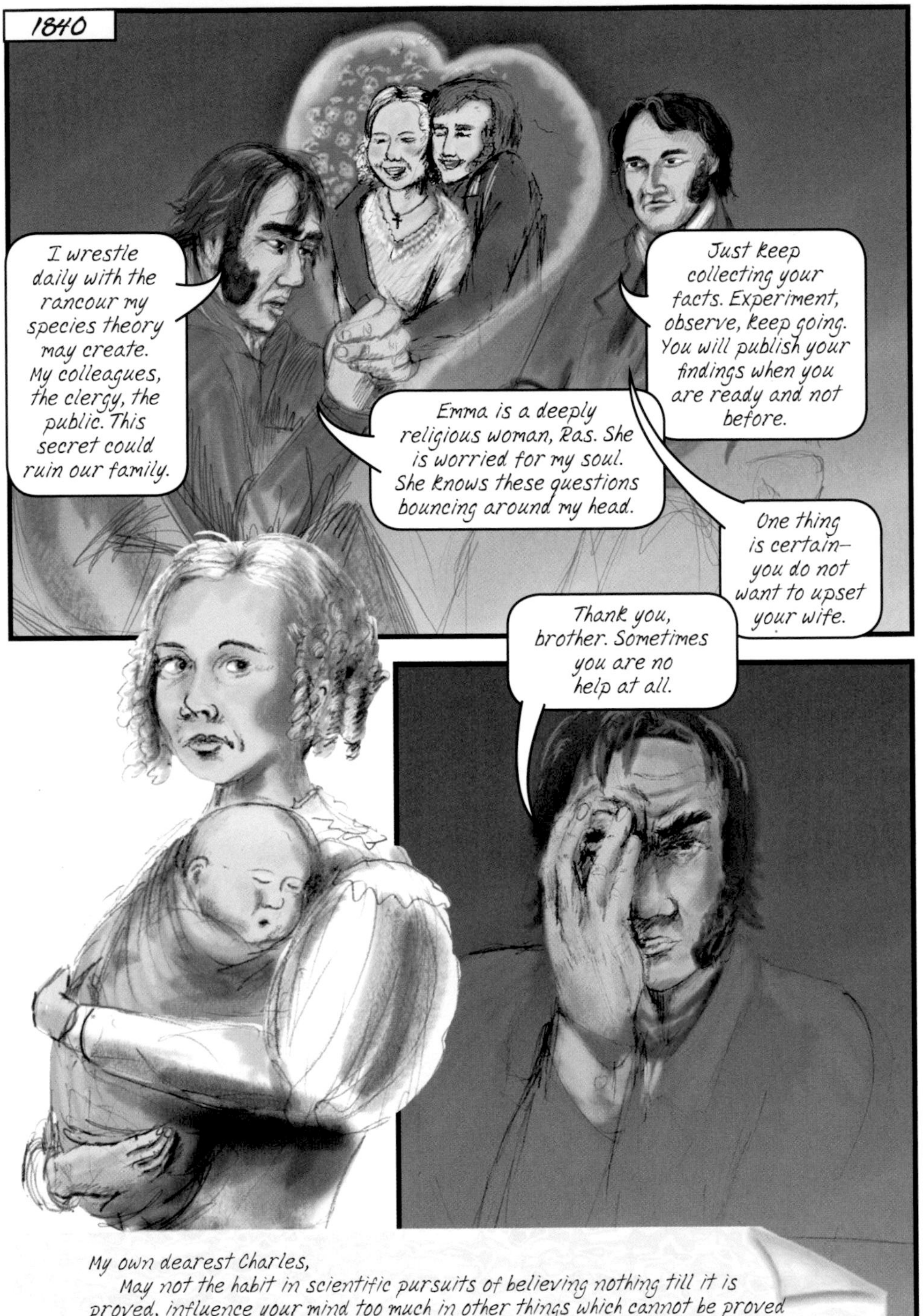
1840
I wrestle daily with the rancour my species theory may create. My colleagues, the clergy, the public. This secret could ruin our family.
Emma is a deeply religious woman, Ras. She is worried for my soul. She knows these questions bouncing around my head.
Just keep collecting your facts. Experiment, observe, keep going. You will publish your findings when you are ready and not before.
One thing is certain— you do not want to upset your wife.
Thank you, brother. Sometimes you are no help at all.
My own dearest Charles,
May not the habit in scientific pursuits of believing nothing till it is proved, influence your mind too much in other things which cannot be proved in the same way, & which if true are likely to be above our comprehension... Don't think that it is not my affair & that it does not much signify to me. Every thing that concerns you concerns me & I should be most unhappy if I thought we did not belong to each other forever.
Emma

I am very weak & can write little. My nervous system has failed & I am kept going only by repeated doses of brandy.

It is exceedingly difficult to know whether the patient may have been exposed to a tropical illness during his world travels that is staying with him, or whether his mind is forcing this state of invalidism upon his body.

He complains of heaving and vomiting. He is afflicted with severe headaches. His skin breaks out in boils. He sometimes suffers depression, exhaustion, and is bedridden for long periods. Yet he says these symptoms inflame with the stresses of being social and when his mind is laden with work.

My stomach as usual has been my enemy—but Dr. Holland tells me he thinks it is only secondarily affected—and that some other wheel works badly. I have been obliged to give up all geological work, which is no slight mortification, but I hope soon to set to work again. If I had had my health, I should have published my coral volume before this time.

27

1842

WATCH IT

Alms, Ai

PLEASE SIR

VM! STREET APPLES FOR SALE! NNNNNNY INCCHIN! WAAAAAAM SSSSQUEEEAK CCCCCLLANG!

STRESSES OF LIFE IN THE CITY FINALLY PROMPT CHANGE FOR DARWIN AND FAMILY.

A NEW HOME IN THE COUNTRY, DOWN, KENT

The charm of the place to me is that almost every field is intersected (as alas is ours) by one or more foot-paths—I never saw so many walks in any other country—The country is extraordinarily rural & quiet with narrow lanes & high hedges & hardly any ruts— It is really surprising to think London is only 16 miles off.... It is the quietest country I ever lived in & I fear must be very dull to all visitors, as it is scarcely possible to take any drives.

THE COUNTRY ESTATE TOTALED 19 ACRES AND WAS CALLED DOWN HOUSE.

WITH DARWIN NOW FREE OF SOCIAL RESPONSI-
BILITIES, THE THEORY CONTINUES TO DEVELOP.

1844

For now, I shall keep my species theory to only my friends and family, who will rightly tell me whether I have gone insane.

My Dear Sir,

I have been now ever since my return engaged in a very presumptuous work & which I know no one individual who would not say a very foolish one.

I was so struck with the distribution of the Galápagos organisms, and with the character of the American fossil mammifers, that I determined to collect blindly every sort of fact which could bear any way on what are species.

I have read heaps of agricultural and horticultural books, and have never ceased collecting facts.

At last gleams of light have come, & I am almost convinced (quite contrary to the opinion I started with) that species are not (it is like confessing a murder) immutable.

I think I have found out (here's presumption!) the simple way by which species become exquisitely adapted to various ends.

JOSEPH DALTON HOOKER,
BOTANIST AND FRIEND

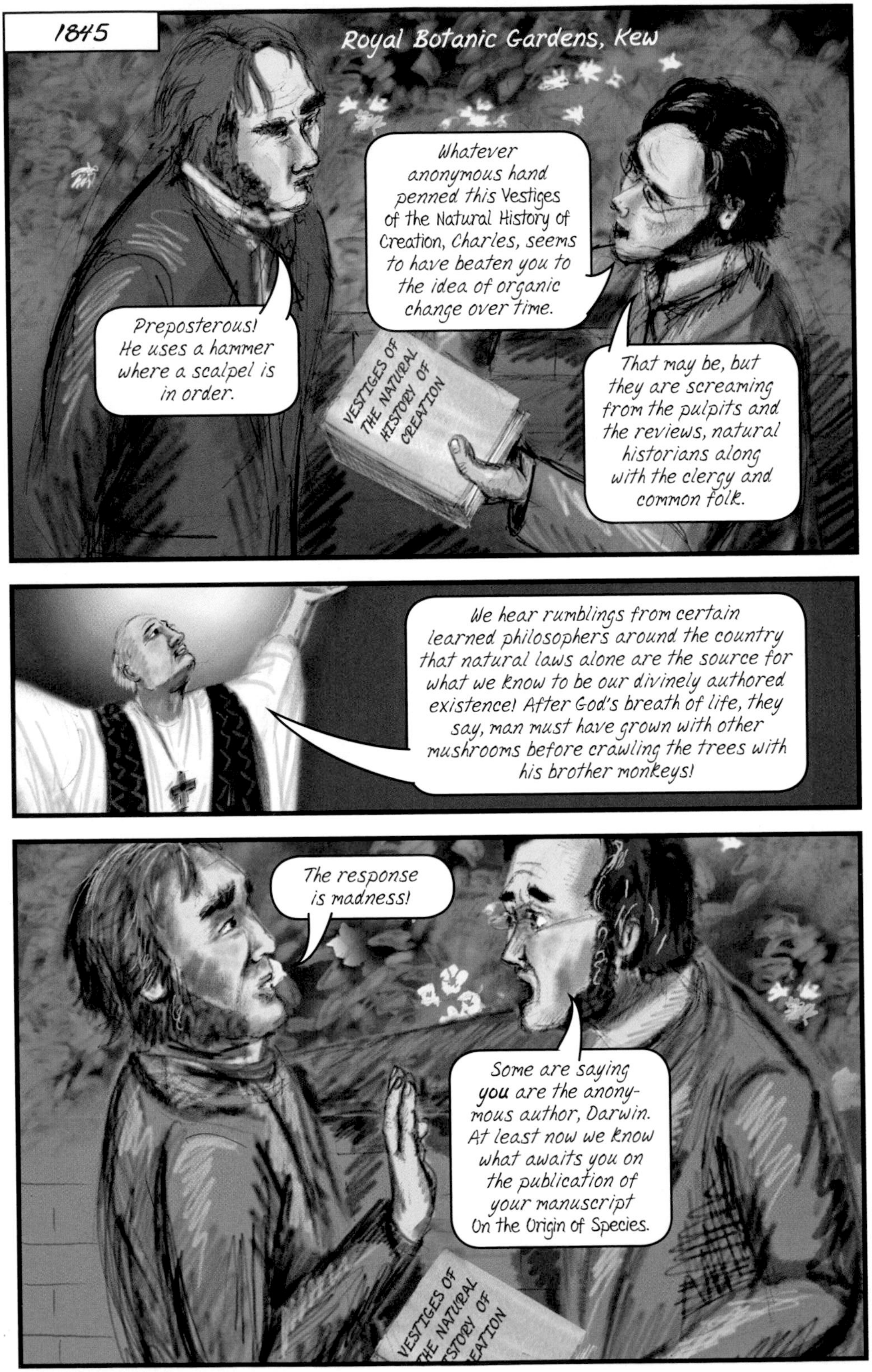
1845
Royal Botanic Gardens, Kew
Whatever anonymous hand penned this Vestiges of the Natural History of Creation, Charles, seems to have beaten you to the idea of organic change over time.
Preposterous! He uses a hammer where a scalpel is in order.
VESTIGES OF THE NATURAL HISTORY OF CREATION
That may be, but they are screaming from the pulpits and the reviews, natural historians along with the clergy and common folk.
We hear rumblings from certain learned philosophers around the country that natural laws alone are the source for what we know to be our divinely authored existence! After God's breath of life, they say, man must have grown with other mushrooms before crawling the trees with his brother monkeys!
The response is madness!
Some are saying **you** are the anonymous author, Darwin. At least now we know what awaits you on the publication of your manuscript On the Origin of Species.

DARWIN'S BELOVED DAUGHTER ANNE DIED AT THE AGE OF 10.

FASTER, PAPA, FASTER!!

I cannot sleep or read or work without seeing a different order to the world from that which I have been taught. I think only of my daughter and my idea.

She was my favourite child; her cordiality, openness, buoyant joyousness & strong affection made her most loveable. Poor dear little soul. Well it is all over...

Whence does this life come?

To where does it go?

DINNER WITH MENTOR AND FRIEND CHARLES LYELL

Yet still you digest this idea without letting the world know. How can you know it is good without someone else trying to punch holes in it?

It's not ready. More supporting evidence is flowing in to Down almost daily from around the world.

BUT NOT YET. FIRST AN EIGHT-YEAR STUDY OF MARINE BARNACLES, WITH A HUGE BREAKTHROUGH FROM A TINY CREATURE.

This theory of yours may need more time to ferment, dear man, but do not let it turn into vinegar in your mind. I know great thoughts are often found at the end of those meandering streams of logic, but for your own good, publish and get it out!

What's happened to the male parts? Are these parasites in fact small males waiting to provide their spermatozoa to a female?! Like two little husbands in the wife's pocket. Amazing!

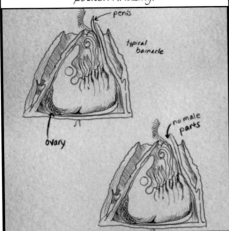

penis

typical barnacle

no male parts

ovary

These different species of Cirripedia suggest the transition from hermaphrodite to a unisexual variant of barnacle! Transmutation spelled out! What news!

This could prove a major step forward in understanding species change and my idea of common ancestry.

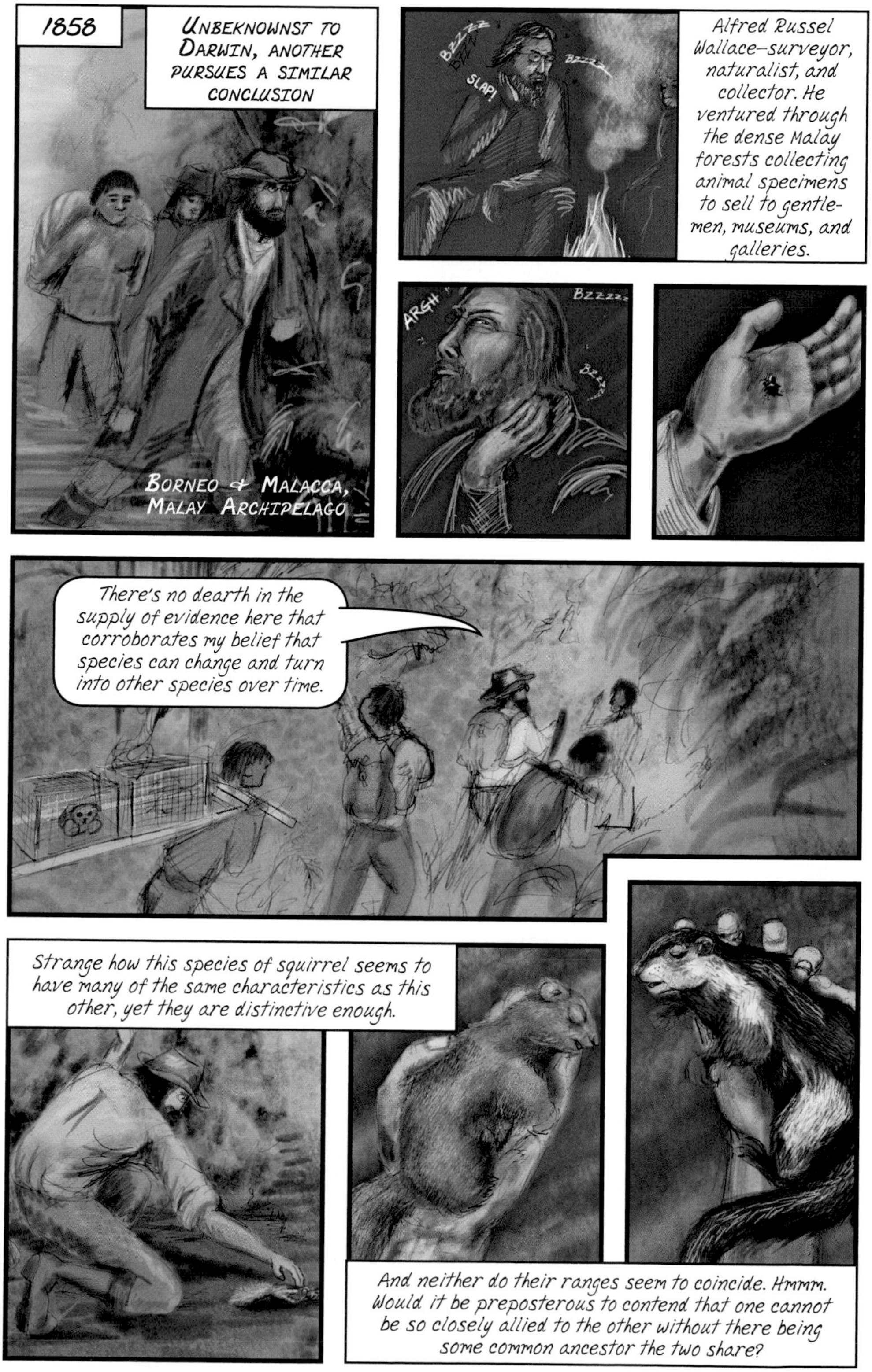
1858
UNBEKNOWNST TO DARWIN, ANOTHER PURSUES A SIMILAR CONCLUSION
BORNEO & MALACCA, MALAY ARCHIPELAGO
BZZZZ
SLAP!
Bzzzz
Alfred Russel Wallace—surveyor, naturalist, and collector. He ventured through the dense Malay forests collecting animal specimens to sell to gentlemen, museums, and galleries.
ARGH
Bzzzzz
There's no dearth in the supply of evidence here that corroborates my belief that species can change and turn into other species over time.
Strange how this species of squirrel seems to have many of the same characteristics as this other, yet they are distinctive enough.
And neither do their ranges seem to coincide. Hmmm. Would it be preposterous to contend that one cannot be so closely allied to the other without there being some common ancestor the two share?

After a fortnight one of my servants was seized with fever, and on returning to Malacca, the same disease, attacked the other as well as myself.
By a liberal use of quinine, I soon recovered.

So your fever has passed? Keeping busy, I see.

I have indeed been busy. I've come up with a theory of common ancestry and descent with modification for plants and animals.

I have read the greats— Malthus, Lamarck, Lyell, Darwin. I have taken from their work and expanded upon it.

No one has thought of this before.

I've penned this article spelling it out. I also discuss the common struggle for existence and the adaptation of useful variations to survive in specific conditions.

I intend to send it to Mr. Darwin, for I feel he is one of a few in the position to understand it, and I hope he will forward it on to the proper authorities for publication.

INADVERTENTLY, WALLACE HAD SENT BACK THE MOST IMPORTANT PIECE OF INFORMATION DARWIN NEEDED TO PUSH HIM TO PUBLISH: A COMPETING THEORY OF SPECIES' DESCENT WITH MODIFICATION.

Dear Sir Charles Darwin,

...there is a general principle in nature which will cause many varieties to survive the parent species, and to give rise to successive variations departing further and further from the original type...

Alfred Wallace

My dear Lyell,

Wallace has today sent me the enclosed & asked me to forward it to you. It seems to me well worth reading. Your words have come true with a vengeance that I should be forestalled. You said this when I explained to you here very briefly my views of "Natural Selection" depending on the Struggle for existence.

I never saw a more striking coincidence. If Wallace had my M.S. sketch written out in 1842 he could not have made a better short abstract! Even his terms now stand as Heads of my Chapters....So all my originality, whatever it may amount to, will be smashed....

C. Darwin

Darwin's friends sprang into action to ensure that his claim to the theory on the origin and change of species would not be thwarted.

...I will begin with Mr. Darwin's article...ahem..."De Candolle, in an eloquent passage, has declared that all nature is at war, one organism with another, or with external nature. Seeing the contented face of nature, this may at first be well doubted; but reflection will inevitably prove it is too true..."

MEETING OF THE LINNEAN SOCIETY, SOCIETY SECRETARY JOHN JOSEPH BENNETT PRESIDING

1859

To Mr. John Murray

My dear Sir, I have heard with pleasure from Sir C. Lyell that you are inclined to publish my work On the Origin of Species; but that before deciding & offering any terms you require to see my M.S. My work is divided into 12 chapters, as you will see in appended table at end of this letter.

It is done. My name, while not alone, is now joined forever in public discourse to a most controversial theory—one that says nothing is permanent, where every being struggles to live and reproduce in a savage world and where only the fittest can possibly survive.

Introductory Remarks with briefest outline of whole Book

I. Variation under Domestication; or the origin & mode of formation of our domestic Productions.

II. Variation under Nature (short & dry chapter)

III. Struggle for Existence (short & rather interesting chp.)

IV. Natural Selection (important; parts rather obtuse)

V. Laws of Variation (many curious facts)

VI. Difficulties in Transitions of Organs & Beings

VII. Instinct (Interesting Chapter)

VIII. Hybridism (Long & rather curious chapter)

IX. Geological Succession of Beings on Earth (long chp.)

X. Geographical Distribution of Beings (long chapter)

XI. Affinities; Classification: Embryology

Rudimentary Organs (important & I think good chp)

XII. Recapitulation & Conclusion (Short chapter)

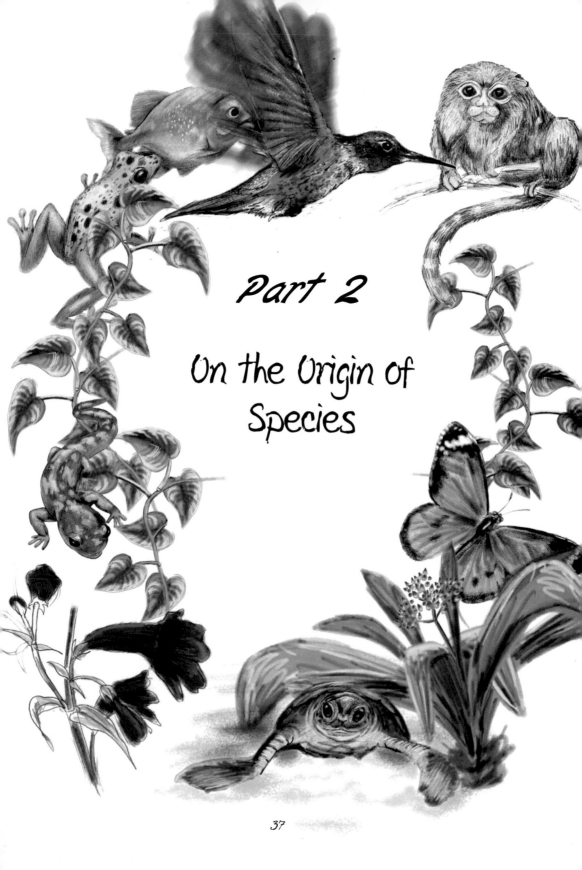

Part 2

On the Origin of Species

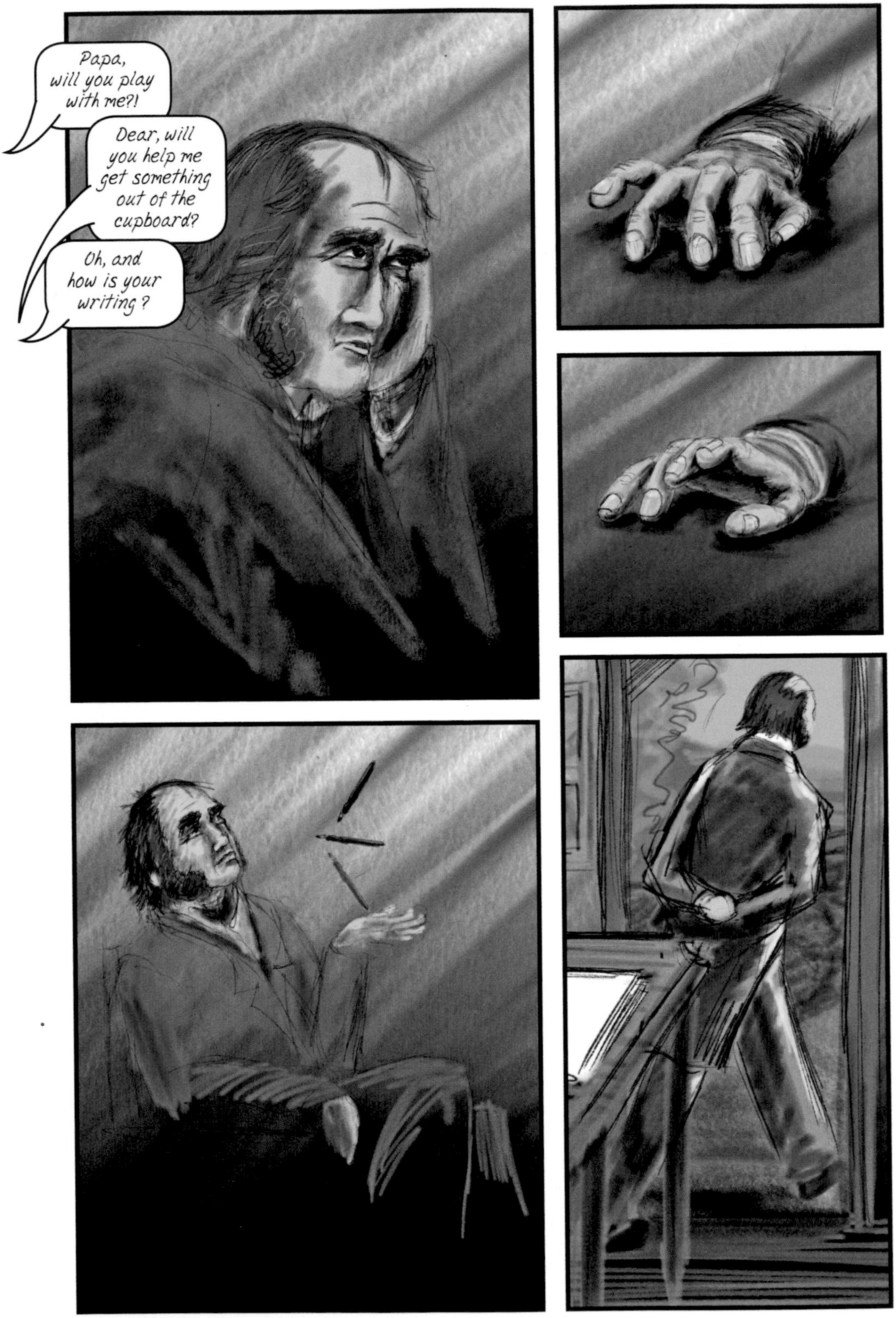
Papa, will you play with me?!
Dear, will you help me get something out of the cupboard?
Oh, and how is your writing?

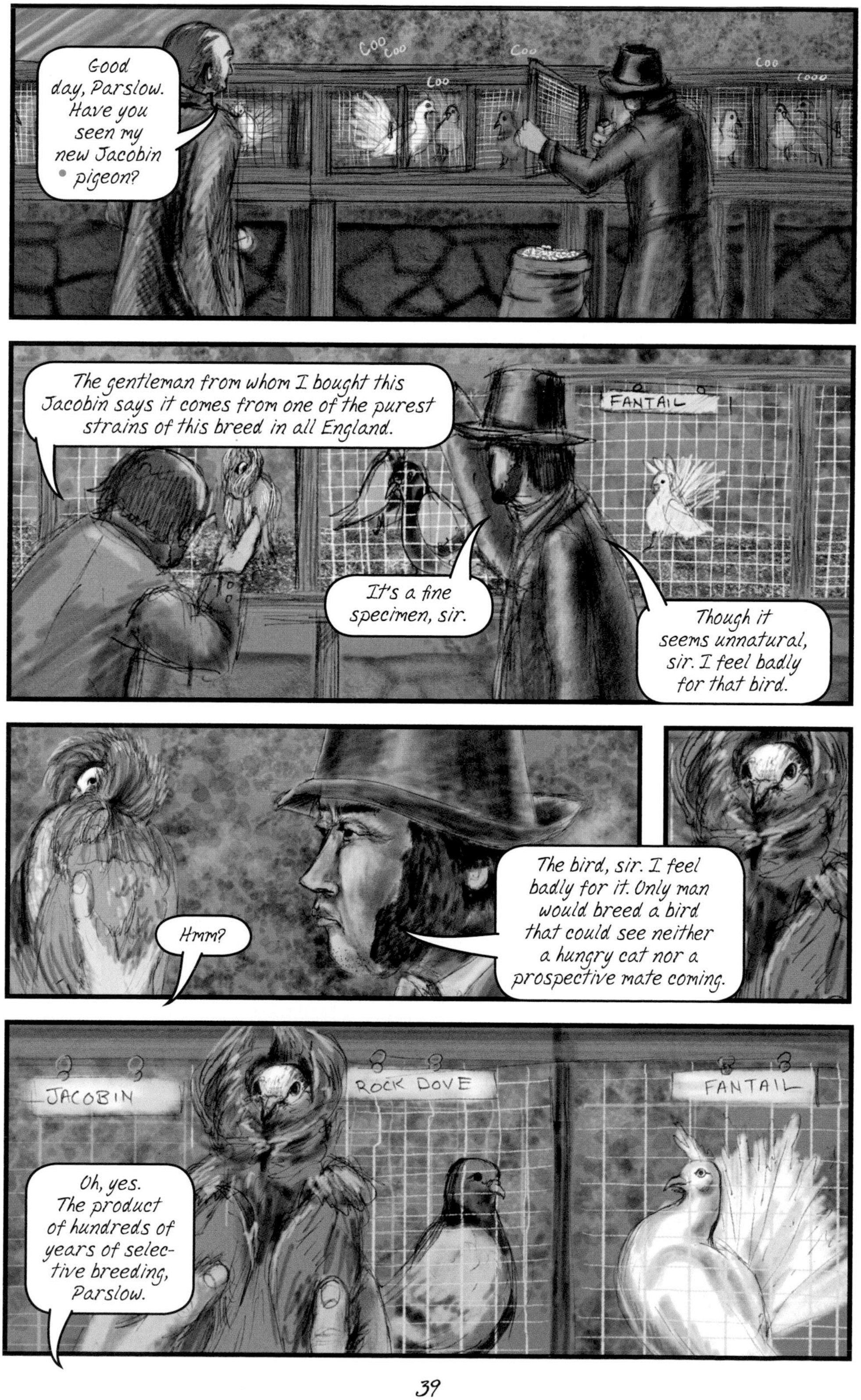
Good day, Parslow. Have you seen my new Jacobin pigeon?
COO COO
COO
COO
COO
COOO
The gentleman from whom I bought this Jacobin says it comes from one of the purest strains of this breed in all England.
FANTAIL
It's a fine specimen, sir.
Though it seems unnatural, sir. I feel badly for that bird.
Hmm?
The bird, sir. I feel badly for it. Only man would breed a bird that could see neither a hungry cat nor a prospective mate coming.
JACOBIN
ROCK DOVE
FANTAIL
Oh, yes. The product of hundreds of years of selective breeding, Parslow.

Look here, sir. Remember how we were commenting just the other day on how the hatchlings can display a wide variety of traits? Even in this breed, some have longer neck feathers, others shorter. And even a few look something like a common park pigeon.

Yes, those are pulled out so they don't mate. There's some type of plasticity at work in the bloodline of the rock pigeon, from which all these fancy birds come.

Yes, sir. Varieties built atop a general form, like carriages.

Hmm. Varieties of a similar form. Should I devote part of my book's long argument for descent with modification to man's domestic varieties of livestock and plants? What better example of the plasticity of species is there? We shall thus see that a large amount of hereditary modification is at least possible, and what is equally or more important, we shall see how great is the power of man in accumulating by his selection successive slight variations.

That's it! Thank you, dear Parslow!

Uh, you're welcome, sir...

First I must point out the variation inherent to all sexual organisms, then I will begin to show that variation is passed on from parent to offspring. I must start with what most will know—our own domesticated plants and animals.

CHAPTER 1

VARIATION UNDER DOMESTICATION

IN WHICH I ARGUE THAT MAN'S PRODUCTIONS OF ANIMAL AND PLANT STOCKS ARE THE RESULT OF MANY GENERATIONS OF DOMESTIC BREEDING FROM ABORIGINAL ANCESTORS. TO ACHIEVE HIS ENDS OF DOMESTICATION, MAN HAS SEIZED ON THE SEEMINGLY LIMITLESS SPRING OF VARIATIONS FOUND IN ALMOST ALL ORGANISMS.

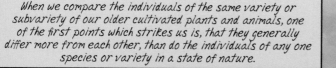

When we compare the individuals of the same variety or subvariety of our older cultivated plants and animals, one of the first points which strikes us is, that they generally differ more from each other, than do the individuals of any one species or variety in a state of nature.

Seedlings from the same fruit, and the young of the same litter, sometimes differ considerably from each other, though both the young and the parents, as Muller has remarked, have apparently been exposed to exactly the same conditions of life.

This shows how unimportant the direct effects of the conditions of life are in comparison with the laws of reproduction, and of growth, and of inheritance; for had the action of the conditions been direct, if any of the young had varied, all would probably have varied in the same manner.

How is it that all your adult pigs are black?

The pigs eat the paint-root, which colours their bones pink, and which causes the hoofs of all but the black varieties to drop off. We select the black members of a litter for raising, as they alone have a good chance of living.

From facts collected by Heusinger, it appears that white sheep and pigs are injured by certain plants, whilst dark-coloured individuals escape....

And we know certain traits are linked to others. Hairless dogs have imperfect teeth; pigeons with feathered feet have skin between their outer toes. This correlation of one trait's selection to another seemingly unrelated trait's appearance must mean that characteristics are inherited.

So the variety in characteristics cannot be caused primarily by either environmental conditions or the relative use or disuse of parts. But how do the traits of parents carry on to their offspring?

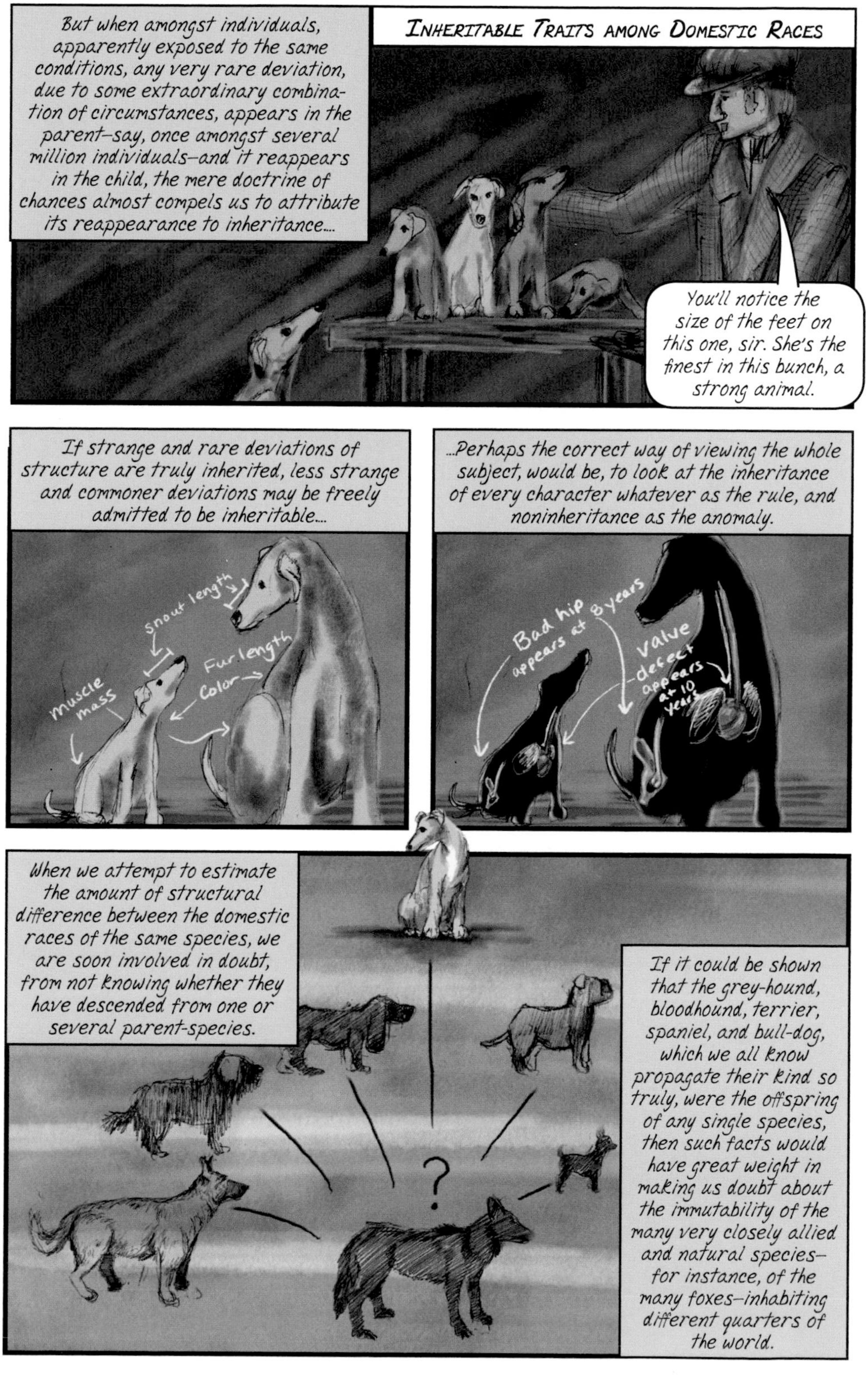
But when amongst individuals, apparently exposed to the same conditions, any very rare deviation, due to some extraordinary combination of circumstances, appears in the parent–say, once amongst several million individuals–and it reappears in the child, the mere doctrine of chances almost compels us to attribute its reappearance to inheritance....
INHERITABLE TRAITS AMONG DOMESTIC RACES
You'll notice the size of the feet on this one, sir. She's the finest in this bunch, a strong animal.
If strange and rare deviations of structure are truly inherited, less strange and commoner deviations may be freely admitted to be inheritable....
snout length
Fur length
Color
muscle mass
...Perhaps the correct way of viewing the whole subject, would be, to look at the inheritance of every character whatever as the rule, and noninheritance as the anomaly.
Bad hip appears at 8 years
Valve defect appears at 10 years
When we attempt to estimate the amount of structural difference between the domestic races of the same species, we are soon involved in doubt, from not knowing whether they have descended from one or several parent-species.
?
If it could be shown that the grey-hound, bloodhound, terrier, spaniel, and bull-dog, which we all know propagate their kind so truly, were the offspring of any single species, then such facts would have great weight in making us doubt about the immutability of the many very closely allied and natural species–for instance, of the many foxes–inhabiting different quarters of the world.

Believing that it is always best to study some special group, I have, after deliberation, taken up domestic pigeons.... The diversity of the breeds is something astonishing.

Altogether at least a score of pigeons might be chosen, which if shown to an ornithologist, and he were told that they were wild birds, would certainly, I think, be ranked by him as well-defined species....

Great as the differences are between the breeds of pigeons, I am fully convinced that the common opinion of naturalists is correct, namely, that all have descended from the rock pigeon (Columba livia)....

Let us now briefly consider the steps by which domestic races have been produced, either from one or from several allied species.

One of the most remarkable features in our domesticated races is that we see in them adaptation, not indeed to the animal's or plant's own good, but to man's use or fancy....

SELECTION THROUGH BREEDING

Just as when we compare the host of agricultural, culinary, orchard, and flower-garden races of plants, most useful to man at different seasons and for different purposes, or so beautiful in his eyes, we must, I think, look further than to mere variability.

We cannot suppose that all the breeds were suddenly produced as perfect and as useful as we now see them; indeed, in several cases, we know that this has not been their history.... Breeders habitually speak of an animal's organisation as something quite plastic, which they can model almost as they please.

Come look at this one. His father was my old stud, and his brother is now employed at that same work for me.

I'm looking for a good healthy male to stud.

By God. He'll raise lambs that'll keep us thick with customers, George. I'll take him.

The key is man's power of accumulative selection; nature gives successive variations; man adds them up in certain directions useful to him.... Man can hardly select, or only with much difficulty, any deviation of structure excepting such as is externally visible; and indeed he rarely cares for what is internal. He can never act by selection, excepting on variations which are first given to him in some slight degree by nature.

Eminent breeders try by methodical selection, with a distinct object in view, to make a new strain or subbreed, superior to anything existing in the country.

You are raising some of the finest Border Leicesters around.

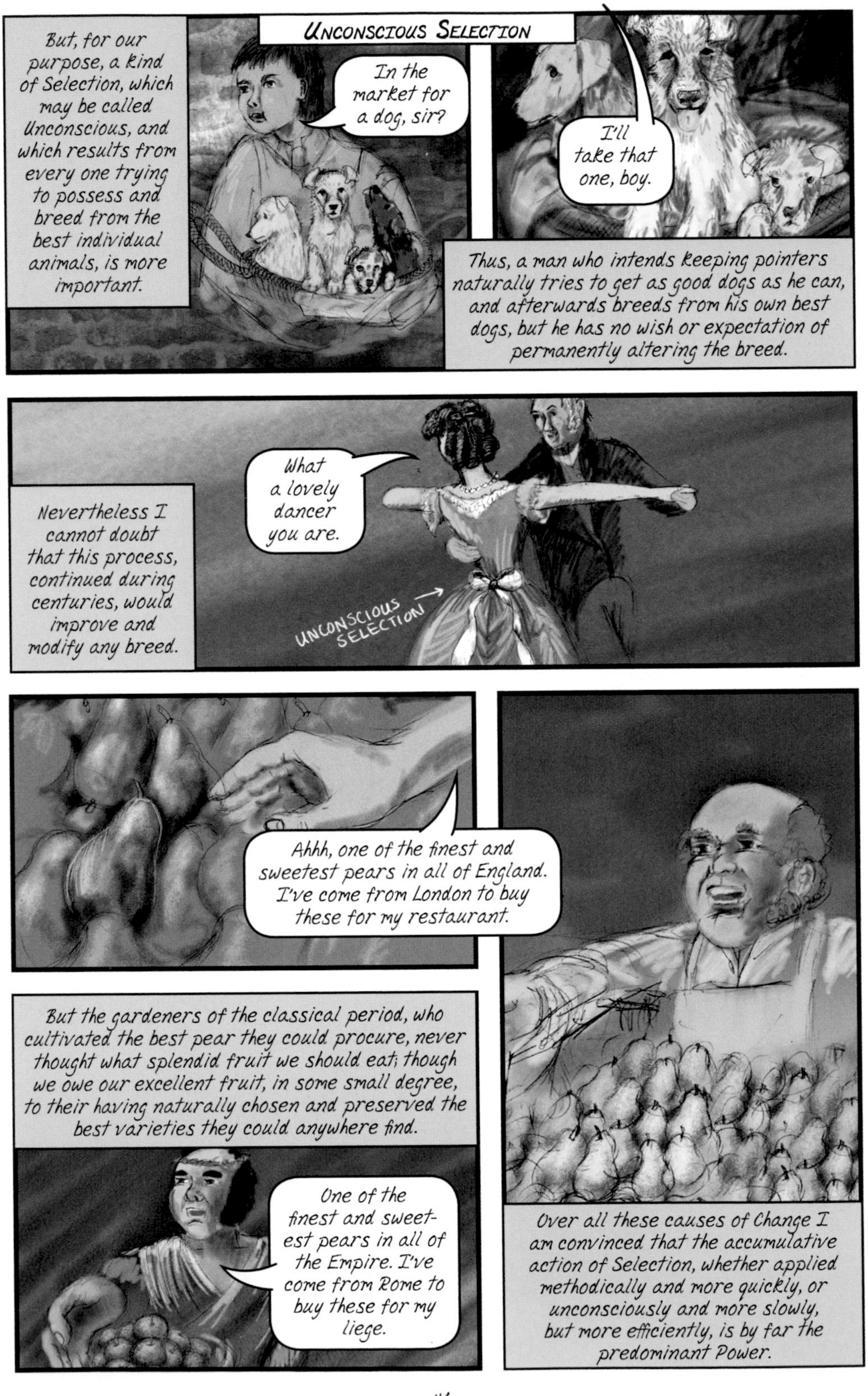
Unconscious Selection
But, for our purpose, a kind of Selection, which may be called Unconscious, and which results from every one trying to possess and breed from the best individual animals, is more important.
In the market for a dog, sir?
I'll take that one, boy.
Thus, a man who intends keeping pointers naturally tries to get as good dogs as he can, and afterwards breeds from his own best dogs, but he has no wish or expectation of permanently altering the breed.
Nevertheless I cannot doubt that this process, continued during centuries, would improve and modify any breed.
What a lovely dancer you are.
UNCONSCIOUS SELECTION
Ahhh, one of the finest and sweetest pears in all of England. I've come from London to buy these for my restaurant.
But the gardeners of the classical period, who cultivated the best pear they could procure, never thought what splendid fruit we should eat; though we owe our excellent fruit, in some small degree, to their having naturally chosen and preserved the best varieties they could anywhere find.
One of the finest and sweet-est pears in all of the Empire. I've come from Rome to buy these for my liege.
Over all these causes of Change I am convinced that the accumulative action of Selection, whether applied methodically and more quickly, or unconsciously and more slowly, but more efficiently, is by far the predominant Power.

CHAPTER 2

VARIATION UNDER NATURE

IN WHICH I EXTEND THE MECHANISM OF VARIATION WE SEE AMONG OUR DOMESTIC STOCKS TO THE SAME VARIABILITY WE SEE IN NATURE. WE WILL SEE THAT THIS VARIATION IN INDIVIDUALS IS THE RAW MATERIAL THAT SPROUTS DIFFERING VARIETIES OF A SPECIES, WHICH CAN GROW TO BECOME SEPARATE NEW SPECIES.

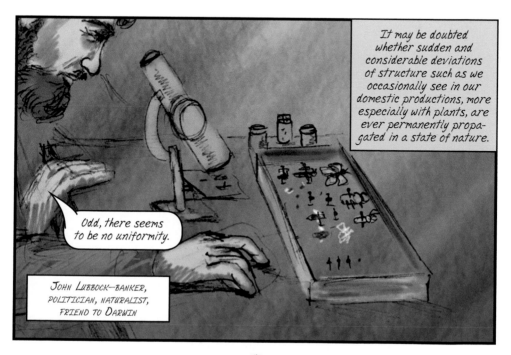

It may be doubted whether sudden and considerable deviations of structure such as we occasionally see in our domestic productions, more especially with plants, are ever permanently propagated in a state of nature.

Odd, there seems to be no uniformity.

JOHN LUBBOCK—BANKER, POLITICIAN, NATURALIST, FRIEND TO DARWIN

The many slight differences which appear in the offspring from the same parents, or which it may be presumed have thus arisen, from being observed in the individuals of the same species inhabiting the same confined locality, may be called individual differences.

Habitat

morphology

Scale Insect
Coccus hesperidum

Individual #1
NERVES
Brain
Ganglia

Individual #2
NERVES

Individual #3
NERVES

It would never have been expected that the branching of the main nerves close to the great central ganglion of an insect would have been variable in the same species; it might have been thought that changes of this nature could have been effected only by slow degrees; yet Sir J. Lubbock has shown a degree of variability in these main nerves in Coccus, which may almost be compared to the irregular branching of the stem of a tree.

15.9 mm

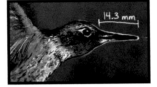

14.3 mm

16.1 mm

These individual differences are of the highest importance for us, for they are often inherited, as must be familiar to every one; and they thus afford materials for natural selection to act on and accumulate, in the same manner as man accumulates in any given direction individual differences in his domesticated productions.

Nectar

Nectar

Almost every part of every organic being is so beautifully related to its complex conditions of life that it seems as improbable that any part should have been suddenly produced perfect, as that a complex machine should have been invented by man in a perfect state.

Many years ago, when comparing, and seeing others compare, the birds from the closely neighbouring islands of the Galápagos archipelago, one with another, and with those from the American mainland, I was much struck how entirely vague and arbitrary is the distinction between species and varieties.

I look at the term "species" as one arbitrarily given, for the sake of convenience, to a set of individuals closely resembling each other, and that it does not essentially differ from the term "variety," which is given to less distinct and more fluctuating forms....

The passage from one stage of difference to another may, in many cases, be the simple result of the nature of the organism and of the different physical conditions to which it has long been exposed; but with respect to the more important and adaptive characters, the passage from one stage of difference to another, may be safely attributed to the cumulative action of natural selection....

Little Blue Heron
(Egretta caerulea)

Snowy Egret
(Egretta thula)

Night Heron
(Nycticorax nycticorax)

Green Heron
(Butorides virescens)

Great Blue Heron
(Ardea herodias)

Great Egret
(Ardea alba)

Hence I look at individual differences...as of the highest importance for us, as being the first steps towards such slight varieties as are barely thought worth recording in works on natural history.

In genera having more than the average number of species in any country, the species of these genera have more than the average number of varieties.

PYROCEPHALUS RUBINUS, VERMILLION FLYCATCHER, PART OF A FAMILY CONTAINING MORE THAN 400 SPECIES. THIS IS THE LARGEST FAMILY OF TERRESTRIAL VERTEBRATES ON EARTH.

We have, also, seen that it is the most flourishing or dominant species of the larger genera within each class which on an average yield the greatest number of varieties; and varieties, as we shall hereafter see, tend to become converted into new and distinct species.

Flycatcher Occurrence

Map based on biodiversity occurrence data provided by: Catalogue of Life: 2007 Annual Checklist: Species 2000 & ITIS Catalogue of Life Hierarchy, Edition 1 (2007) (Accessed through GBIF Data Portal, www.gbif.org, January 14, 2007)

The forms of life throughout the universe become divided into groups subordinate to groups.

CHAPTER 3

STRUGGLE FOR EXISTENCE

EVERY GENERATION OF ORGANISMS SEES MORE BORN THAN THERE ARE RESOURCES AVAILABLE TO SUPPORT ALL, LEADING TO COMPETITION IN THE GAME OF SURVIVAL AMONG THOSE WITHIN SPECIES, AND, TO A LESSER DEGREE, BETWEEN INDIVIDUALS IN DIFFERENT SPECIES.

Amongst organic beings in a state of nature there is some individual variability: indeed I am not aware that this has ever been disputed.

But the mere existence of individual variability and of some few well-marked varieties, though necessary as the foundation for the work, helps us but little in understanding how species arise in nature.

How have all those exquisite adaptations of one part of the organisation to another part, and to the conditions of life, and of one organic being to another being, been perfected?

We see these beautiful co-adaptations most plainly in the woodpecker and the mistletoe;

chisel beak drills for insects & drums to attract females

cartilage & muscle absorb shock

2 claws front & back give support

tail feathers buttress

and only a little less plainly in the humblest parasite which clings to the hairs of a quadruped or feathers of a bird;

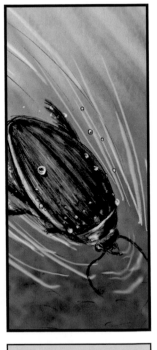

in the structure of the beetle which dives through the water;

in the plumed seed which is wafted by the gentlest breeze;

in short, we see beautiful adaptations everywhere and in every part of the organic world....

But Mr. Darwin, how is it that varieties, which you have called incipient species, become ultimately converted into good and distinct species, which in most cases obviously differ from each other far more than do the varieties of the same species?

All these results follow from the struggle for life...

Owing to this struggle, variations, however slight and from whatever cause proceeding, if they be in any degree profitable to the individuals of a species, in their infinitely complex relations to other organic beings and to their physical conditions of life, will tend to the preservation of such individuals,

and will generally be inherited by the offspring.

The offspring, also, will thus have a better chance of surviving, for, of the many individuals of any species which are periodically born, but a small number can survive. I have called this principle, by which each slight variation, if useful, is preserved, by the term Natural Selection, in order to mark its relation to man's power of selection.

We behold the face of nature bright with gladness...

...or we forget how largely these songsters, or their eggs, or their nestlings, are destroyed by birds and beasts of prey.

We do not see, or we forget, that the birds which are idly singing round us mostly live on insects or seeds, and are thus constantly destroying life.

A MALE CAT'S PENIS HAS SPINES THAT POINT BACKWARD. THE TRAUMA OF THE SPINES TO THE FEMALE CAN INDUCE OVULATION.

FEMALE PRAYING MANTIDS USUALLY EAT THEIR MATES FOR NUTRITION.

A struggle for existence inevitably follows from the high rate at which all organic beings tend to increase.

Every being, which during its natural lifetime produces several eggs or seeds, must suffer destruction during some period of its life, and during some season or occasional year;

otherwise, on the principle of geometrical increase, its numbers would quickly become so inordinately great that no country could support the product.

The elephant is reckoned the slowest breeder of all known animals, and I have taken some pains to estimate its probable minimum rate of natural increase;

it will be safest to assume that it begins breeding when 30 years old, and goes on breeding till 90 years old, bringing forth six young in the interval, and surviving till 100 years old; if this be so, after a period of from 740 to 750 years there would be nearly 19 million elephants alive, descended from the first pair.

ESTIMATED NUMBER OF ELEPHANTS THROUGH-OUT AFRICA IN 2007: 689,671

ELEPHANT RANGE IN 2007

ESTIMATED TIME THE MODERN SPECIES OF AFRICAN ELEPHANTS HAS EXISTED ON EARTH: AROUND 7.6 MILLION YEARS

POTENTIAL HABITAT THAT COULD SUPPORT ELEPHANTS WITHOUT COMPETITION, DISEASE, AND SO ON.

ED NOTE: DATA FROM AFRICAN ELEPHANT STATUS REPORT 2007, BY J.J. BLANC, ET AL.

Even slow-breeding man has doubled in 25 years,

ESTIMATED TIME THE MODERN SPECIES OF HUMANS, HOMO SAPIENS SAPIENS, HAS EXISTED ON EARTH: 130,000–200,000 YEARS

POPULATION

TIME

and at this rate in less than 1,000 years, there would literally not be standing-room for his progeny.

Hence, as more individuals are produced than can possibly survive, there must in every case be a struggle for existence,

either one individual with another of the same species,

or with the individuals of distinct species,

or with the physical conditions of life.

It is the doctrine of Malthus applied with manifold force to the whole animal and vegetable kingdoms; for in this case there can be no artificial increase of food, and no prudential restraint from marriage.

...Cases could be given of introduced plants which have become common throughout whole islands in a period of less than 10 years.

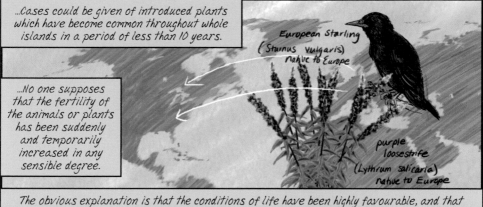

European Starling
(Sturnus vulgaris)
native to Europe

purple loosestrife
(Lythrum salicaria)
native to Europe

...No one supposes that the fertility of the animals or plants has been suddenly and temporarily increased in any sensible degree.

The obvious explanation is that the conditions of life have been highly favourable, and that there has constantly been less destruction of the old and young, and that nearly all the young have been enabled to breed. Their geometrical ratio of increase, the result of which never fails to be surprising, simply explains their extraordinarily rapid increase and wide diffusion in their new homes.

NATURE OF THE CHECKS TO INCREASE

With plants there is a vast destruction of seeds, but, from some observations which I have made, it appears that the seedlings suffer most from germinating in ground already thickly stocked with other plants.

Seedlings, also, are destroyed in vast numbers by various enemies; for instance, on a piece of ground three feet long and two wide, dug and cleared, and where there could be no choking from other plants,

I marked all the seedlings of our native weeds as they came up,

R. bulbosus
D. ouprea
A. Odoratum

and out of 357 no less than 295 were destroyed, chiefly by slugs and insects.

57

Climate plays an important part in determining the average numbers of a species, and periodical seasons of extreme cold or drought seem to be the most effective of all checks.

...In so far as climate chiefly acts in reducing food, it brings on the most severe struggle between the individuals...which subsist on the same kind of food.

...But very frequently it is not the obtaining food, but the serving as prey to other animals, which determines the average numbers of a species....

When a species, owing to highly favourable circumstances, increases inordinately in numbers in a small tract, epidemics—at least, this seems generally to occur with our game animals—often ensue....

LONDON, 1854

THE BACTERIUM RESPONSIBLE FOR CHOLERA, VIBRIO CHOLERAE, CAME FROM THIS PUMP AND KILLED 500 PEOPLE.

...And here comes in a sort of struggle between the parasite and its prey.

Many cases are on record showing how complex and unexpected are the checks and relations between organic beings, which have to struggle together in the same country.

Every one has heard that when an American forest is cut down, a very different vegetation springs up; but it has been observed that ancient Indian ruins in the southern United States...now display the same beautiful diversity and proportion of kinds as in the surrounding virgin forest.

1 year

5 years

10 years

20 years

50 years

100 years

What a struggle must have gone on during long centuries between the several kinds of trees, each annually scattering its seeds by the thousand; what war between insect and insect—between insects, snails, and other animals with birds and beasts of prey—all striving to increase, all feeding on each other, or on the trees, their seeds and seedlings, or on the other plants which first clothed the ground and thus checked the growth of the trees!

We can dimly see why the competition should be most severe between allied forms, which fill nearly the same place in the economy of nature; but probably in no one case could we precisely say why one species has been victorious over another in the great battle of life.

But from the strong growth of young plants produced from such seeds, as peas and beans, when sown in the midst of long grass,

The store of nutriment laid up within the seeds of many plants seems at first sight to have no sort of relation to other plants.

it may be suspected that the chief use of the nutriment in the seed is to favour the growth of the seedlings, whilst struggling with other plants growing vigorously all around.

Plants and animals most remote in the scale of nature, are bound together by a web of complex relationships.

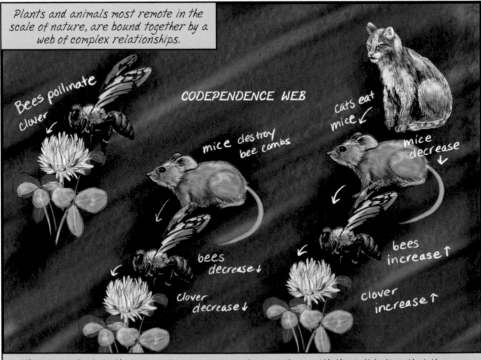

CODEPENDENCE WEB

Bees pollinate clover

mice destroy bee combs

Cats eat mice

mice decrease

bees decrease↓

bees increase↑

clover decrease↓

clover increase↑

When we reflect on this struggle, we may console ourselves with the full belief, that the war of nature is not incessant, that no fear is felt, that death is generally prompt, and that the vigorous, the healthy, and the happy survive and multiply.

CHAPTER 4

Natural Selection; or the Survival of the Fittest

Here we see the variety of characteristics present in organisms gives some a competitive advantage over others in the struggle to survive. The most fit have a better chance to flourish, mate, and reproduce, passing on their successful traits to future generations.

Rock pigeon (Columba livia)

1500

Can the principle of selection, which we have seen is so potent in the hands of man, apply under nature?

1800

Decorative feathers

← Color

← Tail feathers

Pakicetus— early whale ancestor

55 million years ago

How will the struggle for existence... act in regard to variation?

ears developed for echolocation

No hind limbs

nostrils modified + blowhole

flattened tail

Killer whale (Orcinus orca)

Front limbs to fins

37 million years ago— first modern whales

Today

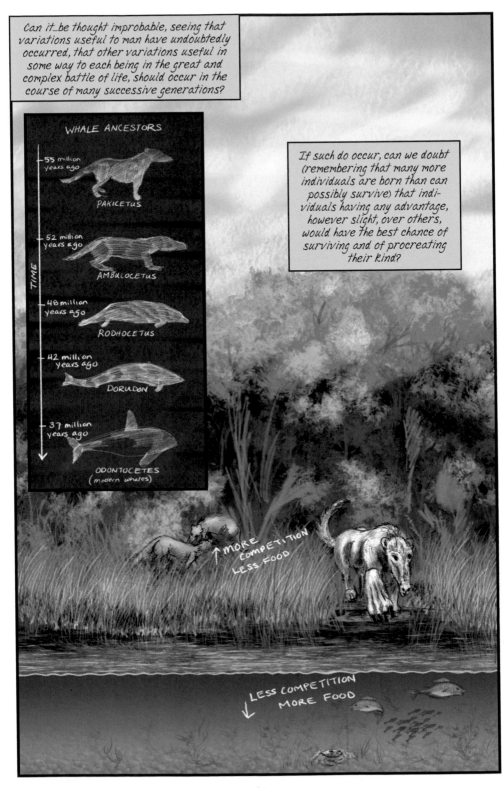

Can it...be thought improbable, seeing that variations useful to man have undoubtedly occurred, that other variations useful in some way to each being in the great and complex battle of life, should occur in the course of many successive generations?

WHALE ANCESTORS

TIME

55 million years ago
PAKICETUS

52 million years ago
AMBULOCETUS

48 million years ago
RODHOCETUS

42 million years ago
DORUDON

37 million years ago
ODONTOCETES
(modern whales)

If such do occur, can we doubt (remembering that many more individuals are born than can possibly survive) that individuals having any advantage, however slight, over others, would have the best chance of surviving and of procreating their kind?

MORE COMPETITION LESS FOOD

LESS COMPETITION MORE FOOD

On the other hand, we may feel sure that any variation in the least degree injurious would be rigidly destroyed.

shorter snout

longer snout

NATURAL SELECTION

This preservation of favorable individual differences and variations, and the destruction of those which are injurious, I have called Natural Selection, or the Survival of the Fittest.

generations pass favorable variations compound

Ambulocetus

...It is difficult to avoid personifying the word Nature; but I mean by nature, only the aggregate action and product of many natural laws, and by laws the sequence of events as ascertained by us.

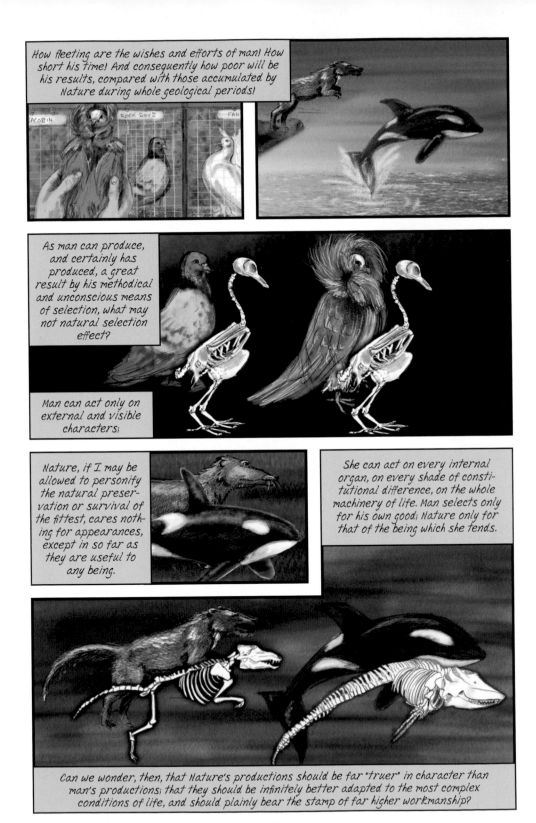

How fleeting are the wishes and efforts of man! How short his time! And consequently how poor will be his results, compared with those accumulated by Nature during whole geological periods!

As man can produce, and certainly has produced, a great result by his methodical and unconscious means of selection, what may not natural selection effect?

Man can act only on external and visible characters;

Nature, if I may be allowed to personify the natural preservation or survival of the fittest, cares nothing for appearances, except in so far as they are useful to any being.

She can act on every internal organ, on every shade of constitutional difference, on the whole machinery of life. Man selects only for his own good; Nature only for that of the being which she tends.

Can we wonder, then, that Nature's productions should be far "truer" in character than man's productions; that they should be infinitely better adapted to the most complex conditions of life, and should plainly bear the stamp of far higher workmanship?

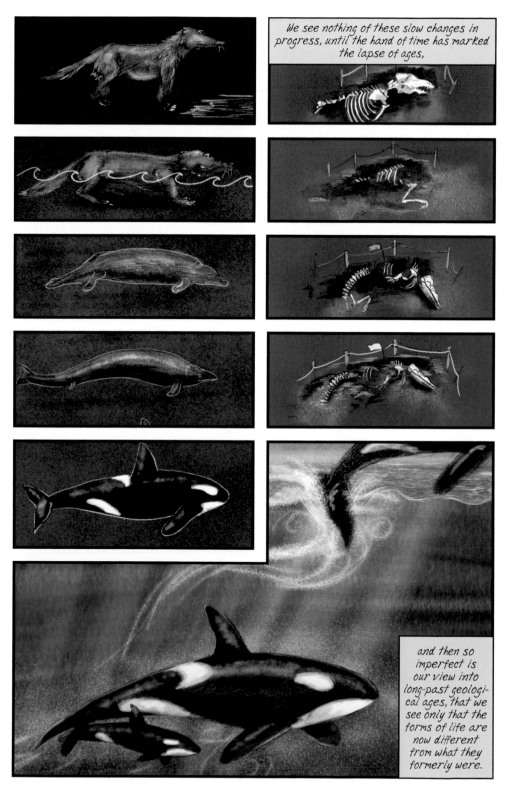

We see nothing of these slow changes in progress, until the hand of time has marked the lapse of ages,

and then so imperfect is our view into long-past geological ages, that we see only that the forms of life are now different from what they formerly were.

65

Although natural selection can act only through and for the good of each being, yet characters and structures, which we are apt to consider as of very trifling importance, may thus be acted on.

When we see leaf-eating insects green, and bark-feeders mottled-grey,

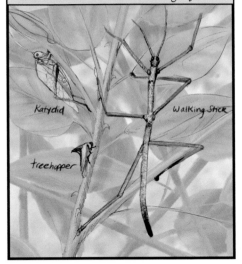

Katydid

Walking Stick

treehopper

the alpine ptarmigan white in winter, the red grouse the colour of heather, we must believe that these tints are of service to these birds and insects in preserving them from danger.

Grouse, if not destroyed at some period of their lives, would increase in countless numbers.

Red grouse
(lagopus lagopus)

alpine ptarmigan
(Lagopus muta)
with winter coloring

They are known to suffer largely from birds of prey,

and hawks are guided by eyesight to their prey.

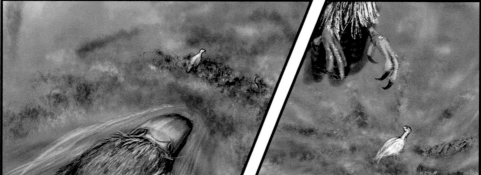

Hence natural selection might be effective in giving the proper colour to each kind of grouse, and in keeping that colour, when once acquired, true and constant.

Nor ought we to think that the occasional destruction of an animal of any particular colour would produce little effect.

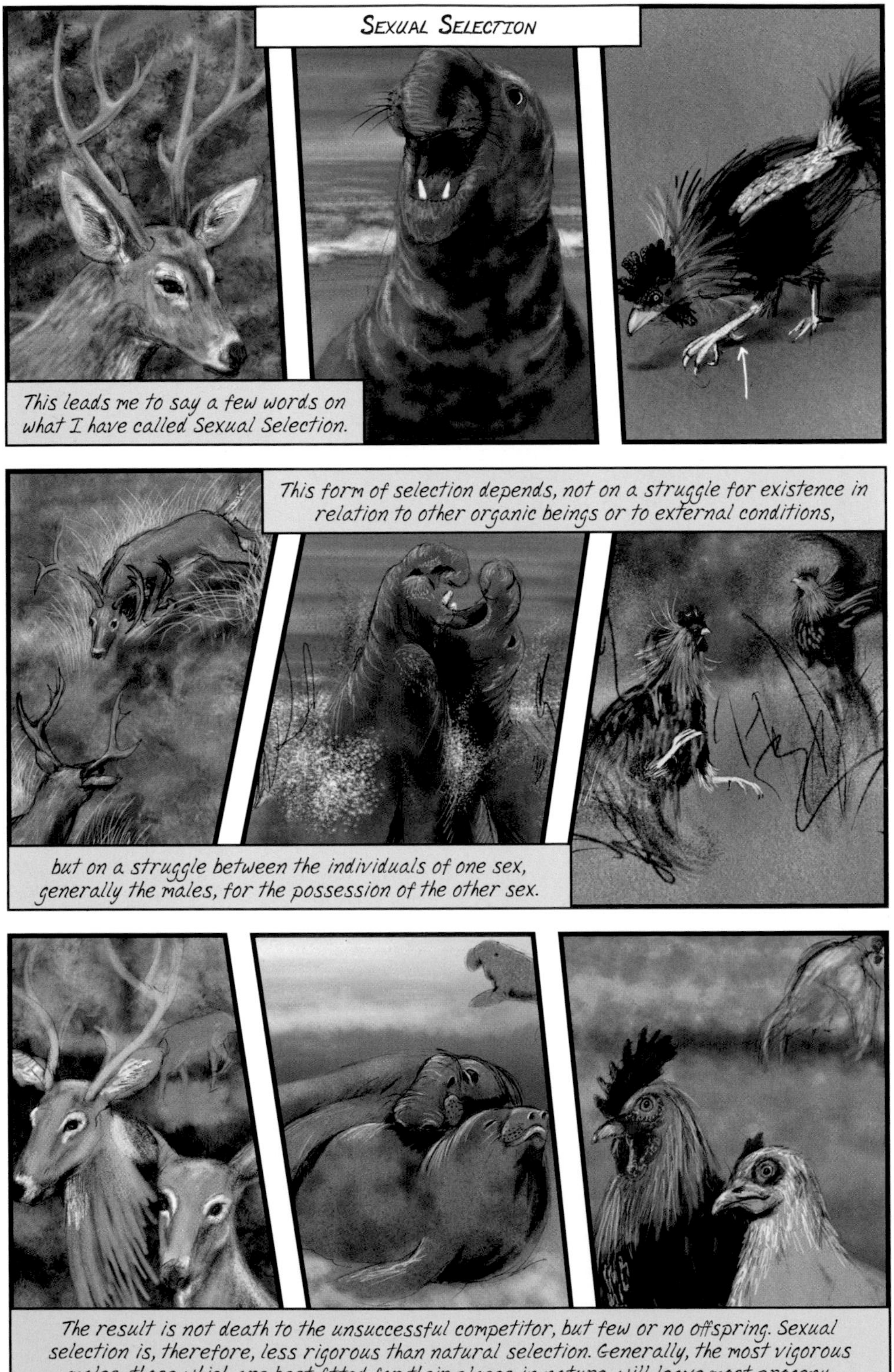
Sexual Selection
This leads me to say a few words on what I have called Sexual Selection.
This form of selection depends, not on a struggle for existence in relation to other organic beings or to external conditions,
but on a struggle between the individuals of one sex, generally the males, for the possession of the other sex.
The result is not death to the unsuccessful competitor, but few or no offspring. Sexual selection is, therefore, less rigorous than natural selection. Generally, the most vigorous males, those which are best fitted for their places in nature, will leave most progeny.

GRANDFATHER

FATHER

SON

Sexual selection, by always allowing the victor to breed, might surely give indomitable courage, length to the spur, and strength to the wing to strike in the spurred leg

in nearly the same manner as does the brutal cockfighter by the careful selection of his best cocks.

The males of carnivorous animals are already well armed; though to them and to others, special means of defence may be given through means of sexual selection,

as the mane to the lion,

and the hooked jaw to the male salmon;

MANE MAY PROVIDE NECK PROTECTION FOR FIGHTING MALES.

A SEASONAL LOWER JAW GROWTH CALLED A KYPE MAY BE AN INDICATOR OF DOMINANCE IN MALE SALMON.

for the shield may be as important for victory, as the sword or spear.

Amongst birds, the contest is often of a more peaceful character....

The rock thrush of Guiana, birds of paradise, and some others, congregate;

and successive males display with the most elaborate care, and show off in the best manner, their gorgeous plumage.

They likewise perform strange antics before the females, which, standing by as spectators, at last choose the most attractive partner.

I can see no good reason to doubt that female birds, by selecting, during thousands of generations, the most melodious or beautiful males, according to their standard of beauty, might produce a marked effect.

70

ED. NOTE: ONE MATE CHOOSING ANOTHER IS NOW CALLED INTERSEXUAL SELECTION.

Thus it is, as I believe, that when the males and females of any animal have the same general habits of life, but differ in structure,

colour, or ornament, such differences have been mainly caused by sexual selection:

that is, by individual males having had, in successive generations, some slight advantage over other males,

in their weapons,

means of defence,

or charms, which they have transmitted to their male offspring alone.

I must here introduce a short digression.

What reason, it may be asked, is there for supposing—that two individuals ever concur in reproduction?

In the case of animals and plants with separated sexes, it is of course obvious that two individuals must always...unite for each birth.

FLOWER POLLINATION

With animals and plants a cross between different varieties gives vigour and fertility to the offspring.

On the other hand, close interbreeding diminishes vigour and fertility.

POSSIBLE RESULTS OF SELF-POLLINATION

BREEDING BETWEEN RELATED INDIVIDUALS

These facts alone incline me to believe that it is a general law of nature that no organic being fertilises itself for a perpetuity of generations; but that a cross with another individual is occasionally—perhaps at long intervals of time—indispensable.

We shall best understand the probable course of natural selection by taking the case of a country undergoing some slight physical change, for instance, of climate.

The proportional numbers of its inhabitants will almost immediately undergo a change, and some species will probably become extinct.

Species C Extinct

°°° Species A

°°° Species B

°°° Species C

Arctic Climate

We may conclude, from what we have seen of the intimate and complex manner in which the inhabitants of each country are bound together, that any change in the numerical proportions of the inhabitants, independently of the change of climate itself, would seriously affect the other.

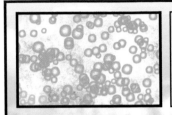

Though Nature grants long periods of time for the work of natural selection, she does not grant an indefinite period,

THE EXTINCT WOODLAND MUSK OX, BOOTHERIUM BOMBIFRONS, RANGED ACROSS MUCH OF NORTH AMERICA'S GRASSLANDS WITH MASTODONS AND GIANT BEAVERS. IT BECAME EXTINCT 10,000 YEARS AGO AT THE END OF THE LAST ICE AGE DUE TO CHANGING CLIMATE AND COMPETITION FROM BISON AND ITS RELATIVE, THE TUNDRA MUSK OX.

for as all organic beings are striving to seize on each place in the economy of nature, if any one species does not become modified and improved in a corresponding degree with its competitors, it will be exterminated.

THE TUNDRA MUSK OX OF TODAY, OVIBOS MOSCHATUS, IS SMALLER THAN ITS ICE AGE RELATIVES, BUT STILL SURVIVES IN THE NORTHERN TUNDRA OF THE ARCTIC.

ANOTHER RELATIVE OF THE MUSK OX, THE BIGHORN SHEEP, OVIS CANADENSIS, STILL THRIVES TODAY IN MOUNTAINOUS AREAS OF NORTH AMERICA.

Unless favourable variations be inherited by some at least of the offspring, nothing can be effected by natural selection.

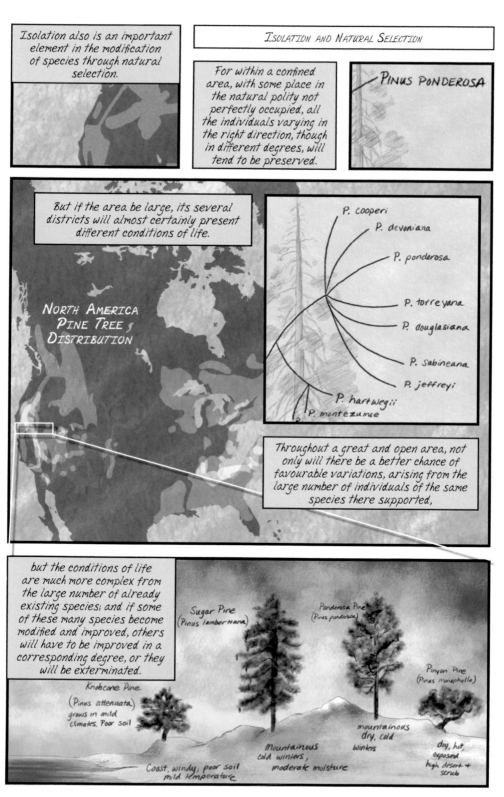

Isolation also is an important element in the modification of species through natural selection.

For within a confined area, with some place in the natural polity not perfectly occupied, all the individuals varying in the right direction, though in different degrees, will tend to be preserved.

PINUS PONDEROSA

But if the area be large, its several districts will almost certainly present different conditions of life.

P. cooperi
P. devoniana
P. ponderosa
P. torreyana
P. douglasiana
P. sabineana
P. jeffreyi
P. hartwegii
P. montezumae

NORTH AMERICA PINE TREE DISTRIBUTION

Throughout a great and open area, not only will there be a better chance of favourable variations, arising from the large number of individuals of the same species there supported,

but the conditions of life are much more complex from the large number of already existing species; and if some of these many species become modified and improved, others will have to be improved in a corresponding degree, or they will be exterminated.

Sugar Pine
(Pinus lambertiana)

Ponderosa Pine
(Pinus ponderosa)

Pinyon Pine
(Pinus monophylla)

Knobcone Pine
(Pinus attenuata) grows in mild climates. Poor soil

mountainous dry, cold winters

Coast, windy, poor soil mild temperature

Mountainous cold winters, moderate moisture

dry, hot, exposed high desert + scrub

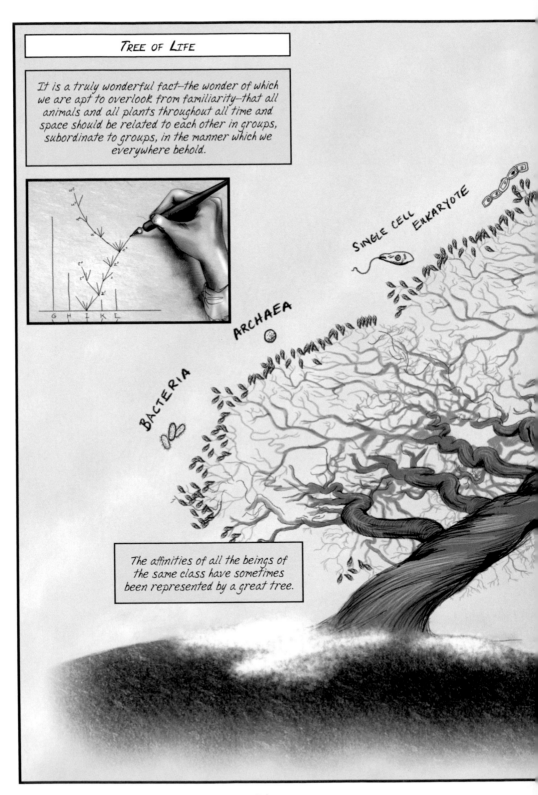

TREE OF LIFE

It is a truly wonderful fact—the wonder of which we are apt to overlook from familiarity—that all animals and all plants throughout all time and space should be related to each other in groups, subordinate to groups, in the manner which we everywhere behold.

SINGLE CELL EUKARYOTE

ARCHAEA

BACTERIA

The affinities of all the beings of the same class have sometimes been represented by a great tree.

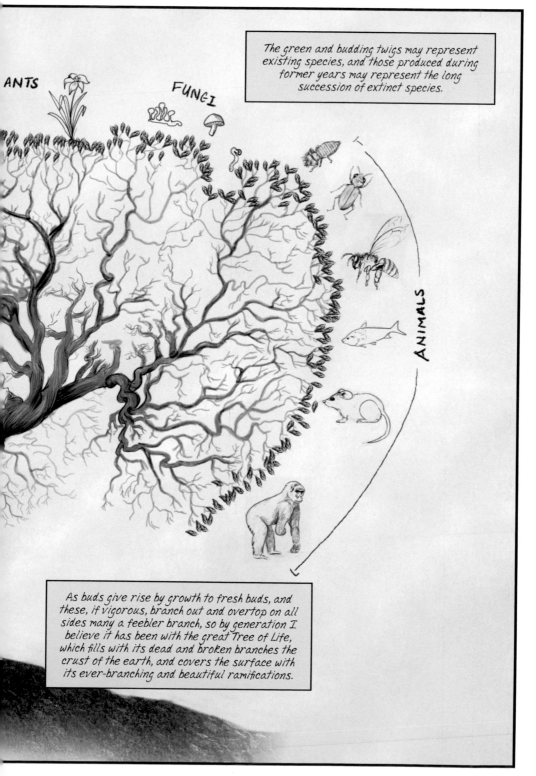

ANTS

FUNGI

ANIMALS

The green and budding twigs may represent
existing species, and those produced during
former years may represent the long
succession of extinct species.

As buds give rise by growth to fresh buds, and
these, if vigorous, branch out and overtop on all
sides many a feebler branch, so by generation I
believe it has been with the great Tree of Life,
which fills with its dead and broken branches the
crust of the earth, and covers the surface with
its ever-branching and beautiful ramifications.

CHAPTER 5

LAWS OF VARIATION

In my time, we had no knowledge of the base mechanism driving variation, but I could see there was some law at work regulating the range of forms available to individuals. I perceived, too, natural selection would play a larger role in the development of some bodily structures and virtually no role in others.

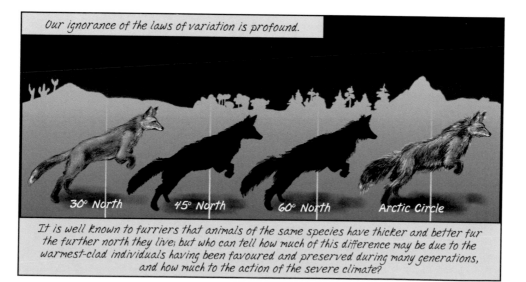

Our ignorance of the laws of variation is profound.

30° North 45° North 60° North Arctic Circle

It is well known to furriers that animals of the same species have thicker and better fur the further north they live; but who can tell how much of this difference may be due to the warmest-clad individuals having been favoured and preserved during many generations, and how much to the action of the severe climate?

In all cases [OF VARIATION] there are two factors, the nature of the organism, which is much the most important of the two, and the nature of the conditions.

Under free nature, we have no standard of comparison, by which to judge of the effects of long-continued use or disuse, for we know not the parent-forms; but many animals possess structures which can be best explained by the effects of disuse.

The ostrich indeed inhabits continents, and is exposed to danger from which it cannot escape by flight,

NORTH AFRICAN OSTRICH (STRUTHIO CAMELUS CAMELUS)

CAN RUN UP TO 70 KM (43 MILES) AN HOUR—FASTEST ANIMAL ON TWO LEGS

but it can defend itself by kicking its enemies, as efficiently as many quadrupeds.

We may believe that the progenitor of the ostrich genus had habits like those of the bustard, and that, as the size and weight of its body were increased during successive generations, its legs were used more, and its wings less, until they became incapable of flight.

In some cases we might easily put down to disuse modifications of structure which are wholly, or mainly, due to natural selection.

MADEIRA ISLANDS— ATLANTIC OCEAN WEST OF AFRICA

Mr. Wollaston has discovered the remarkable fact that 200 beetles, out of the 550 species...inhabiting Madeira, are so far deficient in wings that they cannot fly.

Hmmm, curious.

Hard elytra

ENGLISH ENTOMOLOGIST THOMAS VERNON WOLLASTON

NO Wings

Wollaston said: I never realised this principle so completely as in Madeira, where nearly everything which I have usually looked upon as winged in more northern latitudes was there practically "apterous." If therefore you will grant my premises, that an organ (however essential in some instances) may be variable (i.e. to say, may be capable of development according as required)....

Several facts...beetles in many parts of the world are frequently blown to sea and perish.

Beetles in Madeira, as observed by Mr. Wollaston, lie much concealed, until the wind lulls and the sun shines.

The proportion of wingless beetles is larger on the exposed [nearby] Desertas [Islands] than in Madeira itself.

These several considerations make me believe that the wingless condition of so many Madeira beetles is mainly due to the action of natural selection, combined probably with disuse, like the ostrich.

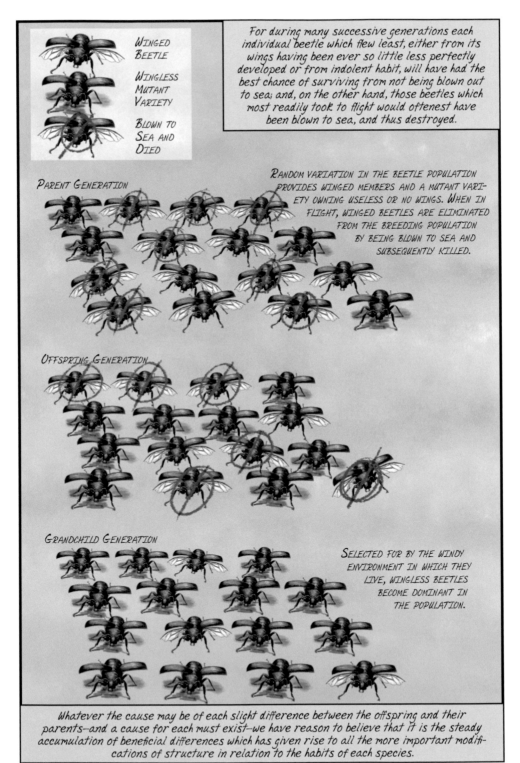

WINGED BEETLE

WINGLESS MUTANT VARIETY

BLOWN TO SEA AND DIED

For during many successive generations each individual beetle which flew least, either from its wings having been ever so little less perfectly developed or from indolent habit, will have had the best chance of surviving from not being blown out to sea; and, on the other hand, those beetles which most readily took to flight would oftenest have been blown to sea, and thus destroyed.

PARENT GENERATION

RANDOM VARIATION IN THE BEETLE POPULATION PROVIDES WINGED MEMBERS AND A MUTANT VARIETY OWNING USELESS OR NO WINGS. WHEN IN FLIGHT, WINGED BEETLES ARE ELIMINATED FROM THE BREEDING POPULATION BY BEING BLOWN TO SEA AND SUBSEQUENTLY KILLED.

OFFSPRING GENERATION

GRANDCHILD GENERATION

SELECTED FOR BY THE WINDY ENVIRONMENT IN WHICH THEY LIVE, WINGLESS BEETLES BECOME DOMINANT IN THE POPULATION.

Whatever the cause may be of each slight difference between the offspring and their parents—and a cause for each must exist—we have reason to believe that it is the steady accumulation of beneficial differences which has given rise to all the more important modifications of structure in relation to the habits of each species.

ED. NOTE: BIOLOGISTS NO LONGER BELIEVE THE USE AND DISUSE OF PARTS HAS ANY EFFECT ON THE GENES THAT MAKE THOSE PARTS AND IS NOT HERITABLE.

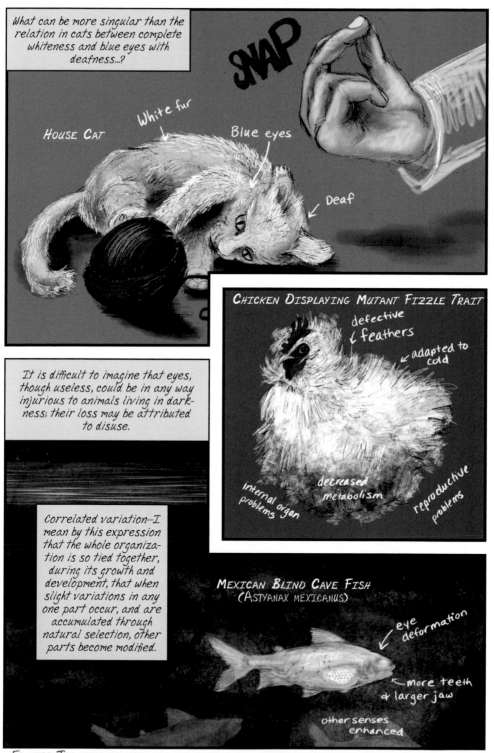

What can be more singular than the relation in cats between complete whiteness and blue eyes with deafness...?

SNAP

HOUSE CAT

White fur

Blue eyes

Deaf

It is difficult to imagine that eyes, though useless, could be in any way injurious to animals living in darkness; their loss may be attributed to disuse.

CHICKEN DISPLAYING MUTANT FIZZLE TRAIT

defective feathers

adapted to cold

internal organ problems

decreased metabolism

reproductive problems

Correlated variation—I mean by this expression that the whole organization is so tied together, during its growth and development, that when slight variations in any one part occur, and are accumulated through natural selection, other parts become modified.

MEXICAN BLIND CAVE FISH (ASTYANAX MEXICANUS)

eye deformation

more teeth & larger jaw

other senses enhanced

ED. NOTE: THE ABOVE EXAMPLES ARE NOW KNOWN TO BE A RESULT OF PLEIOTROPY, WHERE ONE GENE CONTROLS SEVERAL DISTINCT PHYSICAL OR BIOCHEMICAL TRAITS OF THE ORGANISM. AGAIN, DISUSE OF PARTS IS NOT INHERITED.

These propositions will be most readily understood by looking to our domestic races.

With pigeons we have another case.

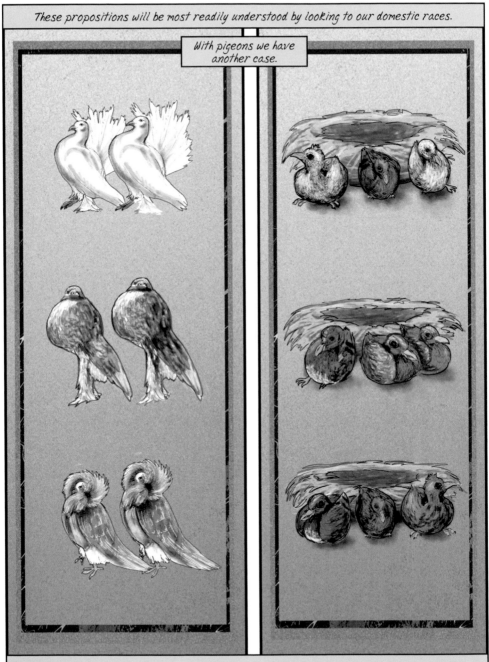

The occasional appearance in all the breeds, of slaty-blue birds.... As all these marks are characteristic of the parent rock-pigeon, I presume that no one will doubt that this is a case of reversion, and not of a new yet analogous variation appearing in the several breeds.

According to the ordinary view of each species having been independently created, we should have to attribute this similarity...not to the vera causa of community of descent, and a consequent tendency to vary in a like manner, but to three separated yet closely related acts of creation.

In this case there is nothing in the external conditions of life to cause the reappearance of the slaty-blue, with the several marks, beyond the influence of the mere act of crossing on the laws of inheritance.

Whatever the cause may be of each slight difference in the offspring from their parents—and a cause for each must exist—it is the steady accumulation, through natural selection, of such differences when beneficial to the individual that gives rise to all the more important modifications of structure, by which the innumerable beings on the face of this earth are enabled to struggle with each other, and the best adapted to survive.

CHAPTERS 6 & 7

DIFFICULTIES OF THE THEORY AND MISCELLANEOUS OBJECTIONS

IN WHICH I TAKE SOME OF THE MORE SERIOUS CRITIQUES OF MY THEORY AND EMPLOY THEM TO SHOW HOW DESCENT WITH MODIFICATION AND NATURAL SELECTION PROVIDE THE BEST FRAMEWORK TO UNDERSTAND THE WORKINGS OF NATURE.

Long before the reader has arrived at this part of my work, a crowd of difficulties will have occurred to him. Some of them are so serious that to this day I can hardly reflect on them without being in some degree staggered; but, to the best of my judgment, the greater number are only apparent, and those that are real are not, I think, fatal to the theory.

Why, if species have descended from other species by fine gradations, do we not every-where see innumerable transitional forms?

Secondly, is it possible that an animal having, for instance, the structure and habits of a bat, could have been formed by the modification of some other animal with widely different habits and structure?

Can we believe that natural selection could produce, on the one hand, an organ of trifling importance, such as the tail of a giraffe, which serves as a fly-flapper, and, on the other hand, an organ so wonderful as the eye?

Thirdly, can instincts be acquired and modified through natural selection?

What shall we say to so marvellous an instinct as that which leads the bee to make cells, which have practically anticipated the discoveries of profound mathematicians?

Fourthly, how can we account for species, when crossed, being sterile whereas, when varieties are crossed, their fertility is unimpaired?

ZORSES, THE PRODUCT OF A MALE ZEBRA AND A FEMALE HORSE, ARE HEALTHY BUT STERILE.

The first two points shall be here discussed. Instinct and Hybridism follow in separate chapters.

THERE ARE NOW MANY KNOWN TRANSITIONAL FOSSIL VARIETIES. SOME OF THEM FOLLOW.

FISH TO AMPHIBIAN

Ichthyostega
365 mya

Tiktaalik
375 mya

Eusthenopteron
385 mya

As natural selection acts solely by the preservation of profitable modifications, each new form will tend in a fully-stocked country to take the place of, and finally to exterminate, its own less improved parent-form and other less favoured forms with which it comes into competition.

AMPHIBIAN TO REPTILE

Petrolacosaurus
300 mya

Hylonomus
315 mya

Limnoscelis
270 mya

REPTILE TO BIRD

therapod

Overexploited niche, more predators

Underexploited niche, less predators

Archaeopteryx
150 mya

Icythyornis
75 mya

Thus extinction and natural selection go hand in hand.

REPTILE TO MAMMAL

Dimetrodon
265 mya

Procynosuchus
260 mya

Yanoconodon
125 mya

Hence, if we look at each species as descended from some unknown form, both the parent and all the transitional varieties will generally have been exterminated by the very process of the formation and perfection of the new form.

WHERE ARE THE INNUMERABLE TRANSITIONAL FORMS?

SPECIES A

SPECIES B

But it may be urged that when several closely-allied species inhabit the same territory, we surely ought to find at the present time many transitional forms.

If we compare these species where they intermingle, they are generally as absolutely distinct from each other in every detail of structure as are specimens taken from the metropolis inhabited by each.

By my theory these allied species are descended from a common parent; and during the process of modification, each has become adapted to the conditions of life of its own region, and has supplanted and exterminated its original parent-form and all the transitional varieties between its past and present states.

Hence we ought not to expect at the present time to meet with numerous transitional varieties in each region, though they must have existed there, and may be embedded there in a fossil condition.

You say these transitional varieties between completely different forms must have existed by your theory. If that be the case, sir, then please indulge us how a land animal, say one with carnivorous desires, could be converted into one with aquatic habits.

EXAMPLES OF SPECIALIZED ADAPTATIONS

It is indeed easy to show such an animal currently that exhibits those intermediate grades between a terrestrial and an aquatic life.

Look at the Mustela vison (American mink)... During the summer this animal dives for and preys on fish,

OTTER-LIKE FUR

SHORT LEGS

WEBBED FEET

FORM OF TAIL

but during the long winter it leaves the frozen waters, and preys, like other pole-cats, on mice and land animals.

And what of the air, sir? In what ways may a mammal take to the air?

An insectivorous quadruped converting into a flying bat is a difficult question to answer, sir. But this difficulty has little weight.

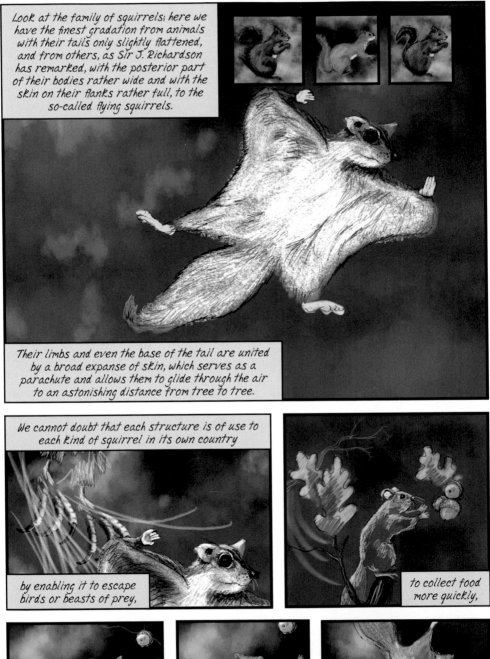

Look at the family of squirrels; here we have the finest gradation from animals with their tails only slightly flattened, and from others, as Sir J. Richardson has remarked, with the posterior part of their bodies rather wide and with the skin on their flanks rather full, to the so-called flying squirrels.

Their limbs and even the base of the tail are united by a broad expanse of skin, which serves as a parachute and allows them to glide through the air to an astonishing distance from tree to tree.

We cannot doubt that each structure is of use to each kind of squirrel in its own country

by enabling it to escape birds or beasts of prey,

to collect food more quickly,

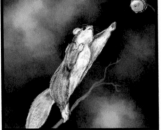

or, as there is reason to believe, to lessen the danger from occasional falls.

Now look at the Galeopithecus or so-called flying lemur, which formerly was ranked amongst bats.

ELONGATED FINGERS

MEMBRANE IS FURNISHED WITH AN EXTENSOR MUSCLE

EXTREMELY WIDE FLANK-MEMBRANE STRETCHES FROM THE CORNERS OF THE JAW TO THE TAIL

I see [no] insuperable difficulty in further believing that the membrane-connected fingers and fore-arm of the Galeopithecus might have been greatly lengthened by natural selection.

This, as far as the organs of flight are concerned, would have converted the animal into a bat. In certain bats in which the wing-membrane extends from the top of the shoulder to the tail and includes the hind-legs, we perhaps see traces of an apparatus originally fitted for gliding through the air rather than for flight.

95

And what of the complexities of the human eye? How can that possibly have evolved through gradual changes when any missing component to the system prevents the entire thing from working?

We may...find aggregates of pigment-cells, apparently serving as organs of vision, without any nerves. (These) are not capable of distinct vision, and serve only to distinguish light from darkness.

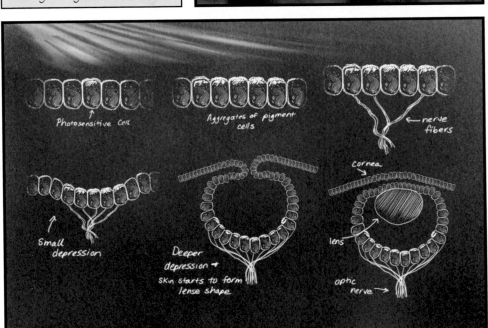

Eyespot

Planaria

Photosensitive Cell

Aggregates of pigment cells

← nerve fibers

Small depression

Deeper depression →

Skin starts to form lense shape

Cornea

lens

optic nerve →

The simplest organ which can be called an eye consists of an optic nerve, surrounded by pigment-cells and covered by translucent skin, but without any lens or other refractive body. In this concentration of the rays we gain the first and by far the most important step towards the formation of a true, picture-forming eye; for we have only to place the naked extremity of the optic nerve...at the right distance from the concentrating apparatus, and an image will be formed on it.

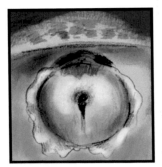

We must suppose that there is a power, represented by natural selection or the survival of the fittest, always intently watching each slight alteration in the transparent layers; and carefully preserving each which, under varied circumstances, in any way or in any degree, tends to produce a distincter image.

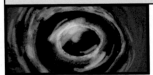

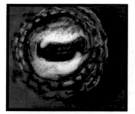

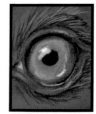

The state of the same organ in distinct classes may incidentally throw light on the steps by which it has been perfected.

SHARKS DO NOT HAVE COLOUR VISION.

DOGS, SQUIRRELS, AND OTHERS ARE RED-GREEN COLOUR-BLIND.

HUMANS HAVE COLOUR VISION.

But what is the process, sir, by which this almost magical change unfolds over time?

It is only magic to those not willing to understand the nature of the change.
In living bodies, variation will cause the slight alterations, generations will multiply them almost infinitely, and natural selection will pick out with unerring skill each improvement.

Two distinct organs, or the same organ under two very different forms, may simultaneously perform in the same individual the same function, and this is an extremely important means of transition.

THERE ARE FISH WITH GILLS OR BRACHAE THAT BREATHE THE AIR DISSOLVED IN THE WATER AT THE SAME TIME THAT THEY BREATHE FREE AIR IN THEIR SWIM BLADDERS. GULPS OF AIR ARE PUSHED DIRECTLY INTO THE TARPON'S SWIM BLADDER AND THE LUNGFISH'S LUNG FOR RESPIRATION, AN ADAPTATION FOR LIVING IN OXYGEN—POOR BRACKISH WATER.

Gills

Swim bladder

Marbled Lungfish
(Protopterus aethiopicus) Gills

lung

The illustration of the swim bladder in fishes is a good one, because it shows us clearly the highly important fact that an organ originally constructed for one purpose, namely, flotation,

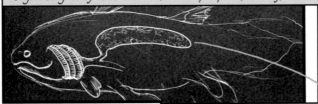

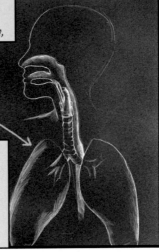

may be converted into one for a widely different purpose, namely, respiration. There is no reason to doubt that the swim bladder has actually been converted into lungs, or an organ used exclusively for respiration.

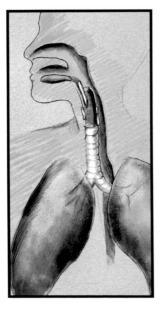

We can thus, as I infer from anatomist Richard Owen's interesting description of these parts, understand the strange fact that every particle of food and drink which we swallow has to pass over the orifice of the trachea, with some risk of falling into the lungs, notwithstanding the beautiful contrivance by which the glottis is closed.

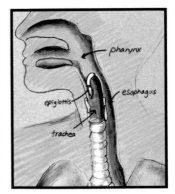

pharynx

esophagus

epiglottis

trachea

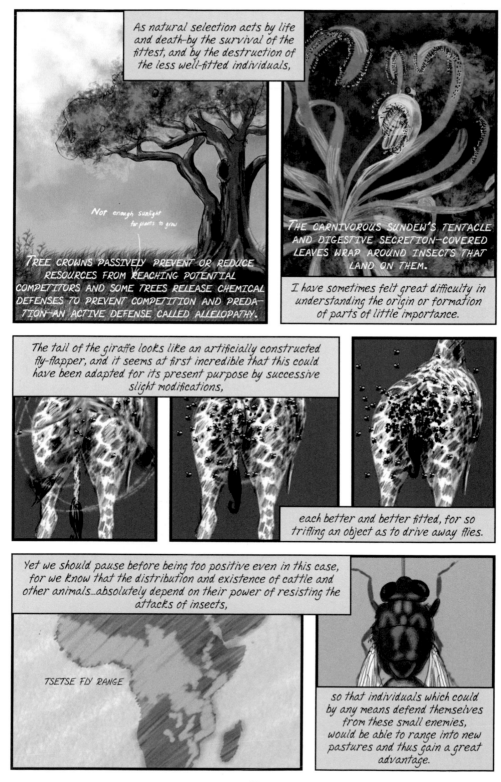

As natural selection acts by life and death–by the survival of the fittest, and by the destruction of the less well-fitted individuals,

TREE CROWNS PASSIVELY PREVENT OR REDUCE RESOURCES FROM REACHING POTENTIAL COMPETITORS AND SOME TREES RELEASE CHEMICAL DEFENSES TO PREVENT COMPETITION AND PREDA-TION–AN ACTIVE DEFENSE CALLED ALLELOPATHY.

Not enough sunlight for plants to grow

THE CARNIVOROUS SUNDEW'S TENTACLE AND DIGESTIVE SECRETION–COVERED LEAVES WRAP AROUND INSECTS THAT LAND ON THEM.

I have sometimes felt great difficulty in understanding the origin or formation of parts of little importance.

The tail of the giraffe looks like an artificially constructed fly-flapper, and it seems at first incredible that this could have been adapted for its present purpose by successive slight modifications,

each better and better fitted, for so trifling an object as to drive away flies.

Yet we should pause before being too positive even in this case, for we know that the distribution and existence of cattle and other animals...absolutely depend on their power of resisting the attacks of insects,

TSETSE FLY RANGE

so that individuals which could by any means defend themselves from these small enemies, would be able to range into new pastures and thus gain a great advantage.

99

It has been argued that, as none of the animals and plants of Egypt, of which we know anything, have changed during the last three or four thousand years, so probably have none in any part of the world.

All naturalists admit that such races have been produced through the modification of their original types.

WILD BARLEY
(HORDEUM VULGARE)

WILD FIG TREE
(FICUS)

AUROCH
(BOS PRIMIGENIUS)

EGYPT
2000 BC

In Egypt, during the last several thousand years, the conditions of life, as far as we know, have remained absolutely uniform.

EGYPT
2000 AD

But how, on the principle of natural selection, can a variety live side by side with the parent species?

CELEBRATED PALEONTOLOGIST HEINRICH GEORGE BRONN

If both have become fitted for slightly different habits of life or conditions, they might live together; and the more permanent varieties are generally found, as far as I can discover, inhabiting distinct stations—such as high land or low land, dry or moist districts.

Sugar Pine
(Pinus lambertiana)

Ponderosa Pine
(Pinus ponderosa)

Pinyon Pine
(Pinus monophylla)

Knobcone Pine
(Pinus attenuata)
grows in mild climates. Poor soil

mountainous
dry, cold
winters

dry, hot,
exposed
high desert +
scrub

Coast, windy, poor soil
mild temperature

Mountainous
cold winters,
moderate moisture

A much more serious objection has been urged by Bronn, and recently by Broca, namely, that many characters appear to be of no service whatever to their possessors, and therefore cannot have been influenced through natural selection.

There is much force in the above objection.

Nerves within enlarged ears are highly tuned sense organs.

In hot climates, enlarged ears help cool blood flowing through them.

Aerodynamically built for seed dispersal.

Some animals use their tails for leverage, others use it for stability or to grip.

Nevertheless, we ought, in the first place, to be extremely cautious in pretending to decide what structures now are, or have formerly been, of use to each species.

8 Petals 9 Petals 10 Petals 11 Petals 12 Petals

As I am inclined to believe, morphological differences, which we consider as important—such as the arrangement of the leaves, the divisions of the flower or of the ovarium, the position of the ovules, &c.—first appeared in many cases as fluctuating variations, which sooner or later became constant through the nature of the organism and of the surrounding conditions, as well as through the intercrossing of distinct individuals,

8 Petals 9 Petals 10 Petals 11 Petals 12 Petals

but not through natural selection; for as these morphological characters do not affect the welfare of the species, any slight deviations in them could not have been governed or accumulated through this latter agency.

Assuredly, being able to reach, at each stage of increased size, to a supply of food, left untouched by the other hoofed quadrupeds of the country, would have been of some advantage to the nascent giraffe. Nor must we overlook the fact that increased bulk would act as a protection against almost all beasts of prey excepting the lion.

graze canopy

graze young grass

graze older grass

Biologist St. George Mivart objects: The increased size of the giraffe's body would obviously require an increased supply of food. I consider it as very problematical whether the disadvantages thence arising would not, in times of scarcity, more than counterbalance the advantages of such an increase in size.

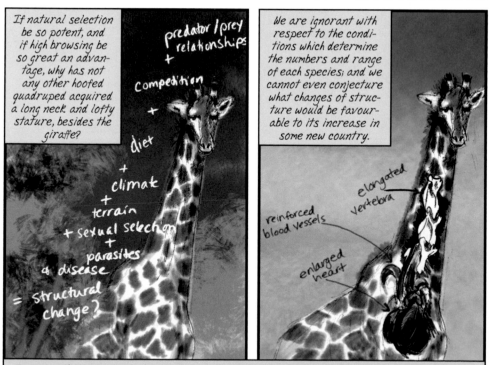

If natural selection be so potent, and if high browsing be so great an advantage, why has not any other hoofed quadruped acquired a long neck and lofty stature, besides the giraffe?

We are ignorant with respect to the conditions which determine the numbers and range of each species; and we cannot even conjecture what changes of structure would be favourable to its increase in some new country.

predator / prey relationships
+
competition
+
diet
+
climate
+
terrain
+ sexual selection
+
parasites & disease
= structural change?

elongated vertebra

reinforced blood vessels

enlarged heart

In order that an animal should acquire some structure specially and largely developed, it is almost indispensable that several other parts should be modified and co-adapted. Although every part of the body varies slightly, it does not follow that the necessary parts should always vary in the right direction and to the right degree.

103

ED NOTE: CURRENT EVIDENCE SUGGESTS THE GIRAFFE'S LONG NECK IS DUE TO SEXUAL SELECTION.

CHAPTER 8

INSTINCT

IN WHICH WE LOOK AT A FEW WONDERFUL EXAMPLES OF ANIMAL BEHAVIOR AND TRY TO UNDERSTAND WHETHER NATURAL SELECTION COULD CARRY SUCH BEHAVIORS FROM ONE GENERATION TO THE NEXT.

Many instincts are so wonderful that their development will probably appear to the reader a difficulty sufficient to overthrow my whole theory.

I may here premise, that I have nothing to do with the origin of the mental powers,

any more than I have with that of life itself.

EARTH BEFORE LIFE

An action, which we ourselves require experience to enable us to perform, when performed by an animal, more especially by a very young one, without experience, and when performed by many individuals in the same way,

without their knowing for what purpose it is performed, is usually said to be instinctive.

I can only assert that instincts certainly do vary—for instance, the migratory instinct, both in extent and direction, and in its total loss.

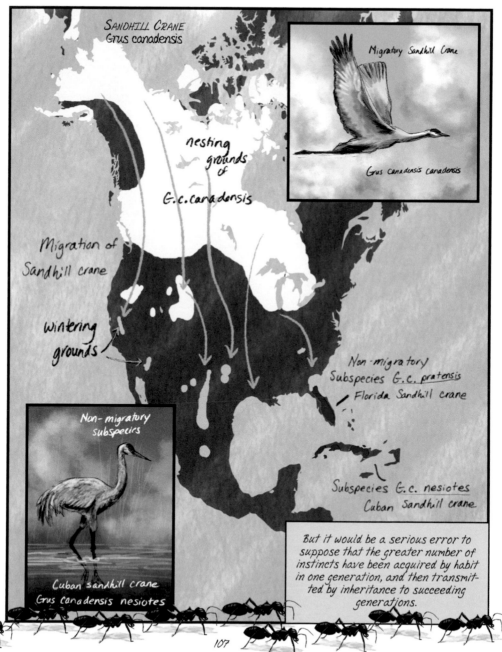

SANDHILL CRANE
Grus canadensis

Migratory Sandhill Crane

Grus canadensis canadensis

nesting grounds of G.c.canadensis

Migration of Sandhill crane

wintering grounds

Non-migratory Subspecies G.c. pratensis
Florida Sandhill crane

Subspecies G.c. nesiotes
Cuban Sandhill crane

Non-migratory subspecies

Cuban sandhill crane
Grus canadensis nesiotes

But it would be a serious error to suppose that the greater number of instincts have been acquired by habit in one generation, and then transmitted by inheritance to succeeding generations.

It can be clearly shown that the most wonderful instincts with which we are acquainted, namely, those of the hive-bee and of many ants, could not possibly have been acquired by habit.

SLAVE-MAKING AMAZON ANT OF THE GENUS POLYERGUS

This ant is absolutely dependent on its slaves....

Though most energetic and coura-geous in capturing slaves,

Slaves feeding masters

it does no other work.

Slaves build and maintain nests

When the old nest is found inconvenient,...it is the slaves which determine the migration, and actually carry their masters in their jaws.

removed slaves

When Huber shut up 30 of them without a slave, but with plenty of the food which they like best, and with their own larvae and pupae to stimulate them to work, they did nothing; they could not even feed themselves, and many perished of hunger.

Without their aid, the species would certainly become extinct in a single year.

HOW DID THIS RELATIONSHIP FORM?

As ants which are not slave-makers will, as I have seen, carry off the pupae of other species, if scattered near their nests,

it is possible that such pupae originally stored as food might become developed,

MILLIONS OF GENERATIONS AGO

and the foreign ants thus unintentionally reared would then follow their proper instincts, and do what work they could.

If it were more advantageous to this species to capture workers than to procreate them, the habit of collecting pupae, originally for food, might by natural selection be strengthened and rendered permanent for the very different purpose of raising slaves.

109

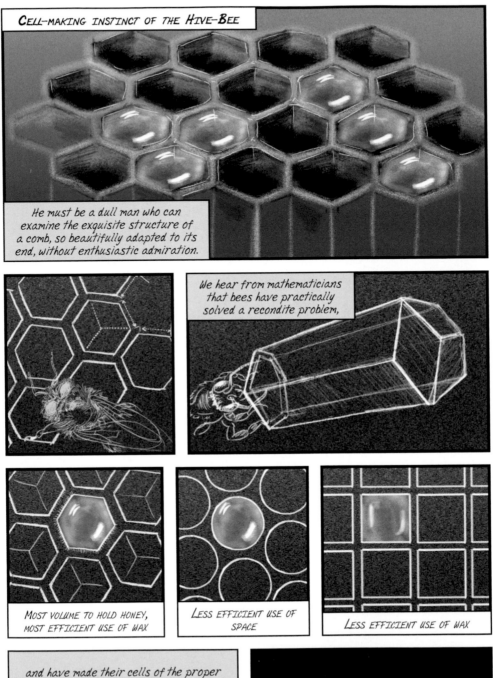

CELL-MAKING INSTINCT OF THE HIVE-BEE

He must be a dull man who can examine the exquisite structure of a comb, so beautifully adapted to its end, without enthusiastic admiration.

We hear from mathematicians that bees have practically solved a recondite problem,

MOST VOLUME TO HOLD HONEY, MOST EFFICIENT USE OF WAX

LESS EFFICIENT USE OF SPACE

LESS EFFICIENT USE OF WAX

and have made their cells of the proper shape to hold the greatest possible amount of honey, with the least possible consumption of precious wax in their construction... an hexagonal prism, with the basal edges of its six sides beveled so as to join an inverted pyramid,...

...though this is effected by a crowd of bees working in a dark hive.

Granting whatever instincts you please, it seems at first quite inconceivable how they can make all the necessary angles and planes

or even perceive when they are correctly made.

The form of the cell stands in close relation to the presence of adjoining cells.

It seems at first to add to the difficulty of understanding how the cells are made, that a multitude of bees all work together,

one bee, after working a short time at one cell, going to another, so that, as Huber has stated, a score of individuals work even at the commencement of the first cell.

HONEYBEE, APIS FLORA

The work of construction seems to be a sort of balance struck between many bees, all instinctively standing at the same relative distance from each other, all trying to sweep equal spheres, and then building up, or leaving ungnawed, the planes of intersection between these spheres.

As natural selection acts only by the accumulation of slight modifications of structure or instinct, each profitable to the individual under its conditions of life, it may reasonably be asked, how a long and graduated succession of modified architectural instincts, all tending towards the present perfect plan of construction, could have profited the progenitors of the hive-bee. I think the answer is not difficult: cells constructed like those of the bee or the wasp gain in strength, and save much in labour and space, and in the materials of which they are constructed.

Let us look to the great principle of gradation, and see whether Nature does not reveal to us her method of work.

HUMBLE BEE, (APIS FLUREA)

Spherical, irregular size and shape

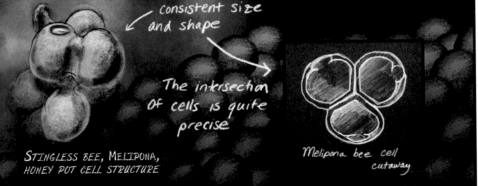

consistent size and shape

The intersection of cells is quite precise

STINGLESS BEE, MELIPONA, HONEY POT CELL STRUCTURE

Melipona bee cell cutaway

STINGLESS BEE, MELIPONA, NURSERY CELL STRUCTURE

We may safely conclude that, if we could slightly modify the instincts already possessed by the Melipona, and in themselves not very wonderful, this bee would make a structure as wonderfully perfect as that of the hive-bee.

HONEYBEE, APIS MELLIFERA, CELL STRUCTURE

Finally,...it is far more satisfactory to look at such instincts...not as specially endowed or created instincts, but as small consequences of one general law leading to the advancement of all organic beings—namely, multiply, vary, let the strongest live and the weakest die.

CHAPTER 9

HYBRIDISM

WHERE I LOOK AT THE PROBLEMS ASSOCIATED WITH THE MATING OF MEMBERS FROM DIFFERENT SPECIES, FROM AN INITIAL INABILITY TO MATE TO DEFORMATION OR STERILITY OF THE OFFSPRING.

The view commonly entertained by naturalists is that species, when intercrossed, have been specially endowed with sterility, in order to prevent their confusion.

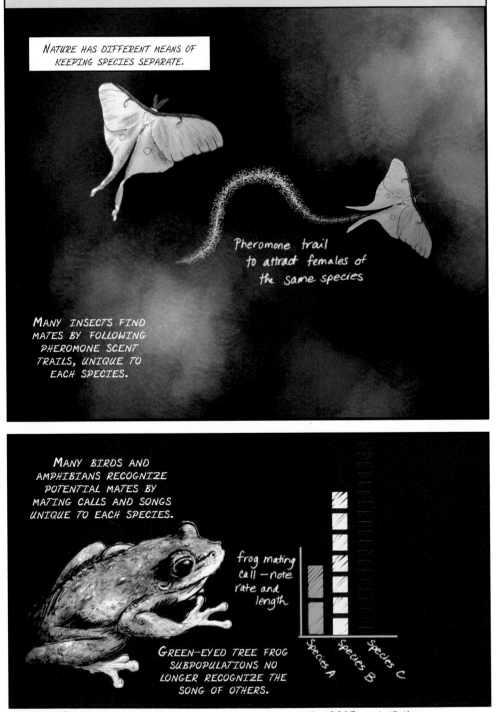

This view certainly seems at first highly probable, for species living together could hardly have been kept distinct had they been capable of freely crossing.

NATURE HAS DIFFERENT MEANS OF KEEPING SPECIES SEPARATE.

Pheromone trail to attract females of the same species

MANY INSECTS FIND MATES BY FOLLOWING PHEROMONE SCENT TRAILS, UNIQUE TO EACH SPECIES.

MANY BIRDS AND AMPHIBIANS RECOGNIZE POTENTIAL MATES BY MATING CALLS AND SONGS UNIQUE TO EACH SPECIES.

frog mating call—note rate and length

Species A Species B Species C

GREEN-EYED TREE FROG SUBPOPULATIONS NO LONGER RECOGNIZE THE SONG OF OTHERS.

ED. NOTE: FROG DATA BASED ON RESEARCH REPORTED IN NATURE 437 (2005) BY C. J. HOSKIN ET AL..

Pure species have of course their organs of reproduction in a perfect condition,

Horse
Equus Caballus

Donkey
Equus asinus

yet when intercrossed they produce either few or no offspring.

Mule
no scientific name

No offspring, sterile

In the case of first crosses, the greater or less difficulty in effecting an union and in obtaining offspring apparently depends on several distinct causes.

Stigma
pollen
pollen tube
pistil
Stamen
ovules
ovary

There must sometimes be a physical impossibility in the male element reaching the ovule, as would be the case with a plant having a pistil too long for the pollen-tubes to reach the ovarium.

The male element may reach the female element but be incapable of causing an embryo to be developed.

Sperm Cells

An embryo may be developed, and then perish at an early period.

Fertilized egg

The results of an examination of about 500 eggs produced from various crosses between three species of Gallus and their hybrids:...In the majority of [these] eggs,...the embryos had either been partially developed and had then perished, or had become nearly mature, but the young chickens had been unable to break through the shells.

HYBRIDISM RARELY OCCURS WITHOUT HUMAN INTERVENTION.

116

CHAPTER 10

ON THE IMPERFECTION OF THE GEOLOGICAL RECORD

IN WHICH I EXPLAIN THE AGE OF THE EARTH PROVIDES SUFFICIENT TIME
FOR THE CHANGING AND DIVERSIFICATION OF SPECIES. I ALSO ATTEMPT
TO EXPLAIN A SCATTERED FOSSIL RECORD BY SHOWING THE COMPLEXITY OF
TURNING A BONE TO FOSSIL AND THE DESTRUCTION OF EVIDENCE BY VIOLENT
GEOLOGICAL EVENTS.

10 MILLION TO 100 MILLION—
ESTIMATED NUMBER OF LIVING
SPECIES

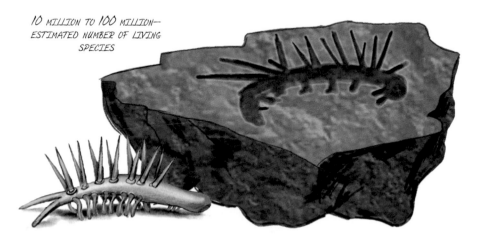

75 MILLION TO 2.5 BILLION—
ESTIMATED NUMBER OF SPECIES
SINCE LIFE BEGAN ON EARTH

Just in proportion as [the] process of extermination has acted on an enormous scale, so must the number of intermediate varieties, which have formerly existed, be truly enormous.

SABER-TOOTHED CATS (SMILODON)

Why then is not every geological formation and every stratum full of such intermediate links?

The explanation lies, as I believe, in the extreme imperfection of the geological record.

Geology assuredly does not reveal any such finely-graduated organic chain; and this, perhaps, is the most obvious and serious objection which can be urged against the theory.

Independently of our not finding fossil remains of such infinitely numerous connecting links, it may be objected that time cannot have sufficed for so great an amount of organic change, all changes having been effected slowly.

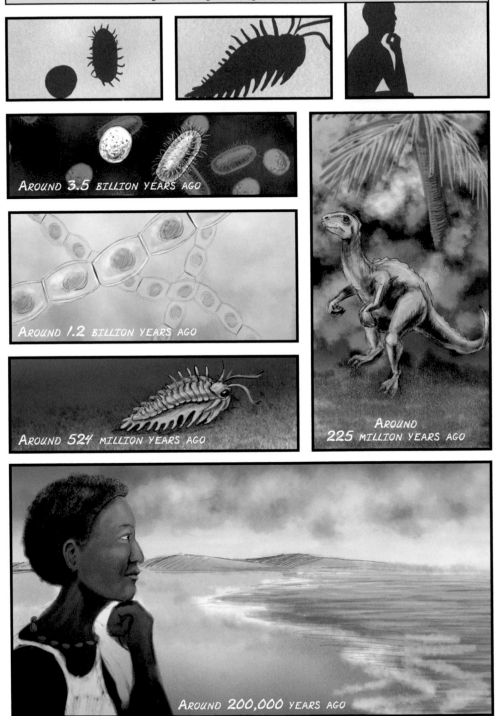

AROUND **3.5** BILLION YEARS AGO

AROUND **1.2** BILLION YEARS AGO

AROUND **524** MILLION YEARS AGO

AROUND **225** MILLION YEARS AGO

AROUND **200,000** YEARS AGO

PRESENT—DAY COLORADO, ABOUT 70 MILLION YEARS AGO

65 MILLION YEARS AGO

A man should examine for himself the great piles of superimposed strata,

24 MILLION YEARS AGO

and watch the rivulets bringing down mud,

10 MILLION YEARS AGO

...in order to comprehend something about the duration of past time, the monuments of which we see all around us.

TODAY

Now let us turn to our richest geological museums, and what a paltry display we behold!

That our collections are imperfect is admitted by every one.

Only a small portion of the surface of the earth has been geologically explored, and no part with sufficient care,

as the important discoveries made every year in Europe prove.

Shells and bones decay and disappear when left on the bottom of the sea, where sediment is not accumulating.

The remains which do become embedded, if in sand or gravel, will, when the beds are upraised, generally be dissolved by the percolation of rain-water charged with carbonic acid.

Though we find in our geological formations many links between the species which now exist and which formerly existed, we do not find infinitely numerous fine transitional forms closely joining them all together.

We can best gain some idea of past time by knowing the agencies at work, and learning how deeply the surface of the land has ben denuded.

Waves wearing away the sea-cliffs...

at last the base...is undermined, huge fragments fall down,...

degradation,...wind,...triturate the fragments,...

frost,...

muddy rills which flow down every slope,...

faults—those great cracks along which the strata have been upheaved on one side,...

ancient formations formed during subsidence...suffer excessively from denudation during its slow upheaval,

Uplift

...with not a wreck left behind.

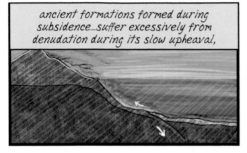

Those who believe that the geological record is in any degree perfect, will undoubtedly at once reject the theory.

I look at the geological record as a history of the world imperfectly kept, and written in a changing dialect; of this history we possess the last volume alone.

Of this volume, only here and there a short chapter has been preserved; and of each page

only here and there a few lines.

Each word of the slowly-changing language, more or less different in the successive chapters, may represent the forms of life, which are entombed in our consecutive formations, and which falsely appear to have been abruptly introduced.

Hallucigenia fossil from the Cambrian era

CHAPTER 11

On the Geological Succession of Organic Beings

Here we look at dynamic species struggling to survive by adapting to changing conditions presented to them. While this continuous change leads to the beautiful branching of the tree of life, we also see there is no goal to species' progression—the branching of the tree is just compounded differential survival of more fit individuals.

No one can have marvelled more than I have done at the extinction of species. When I found in La Plata the tooth of a horse embedded with the remains of Mastodon, Megatherium, Toxodon, and other extinct monsters, which all co-existed with still-living shells at a very late geological period, I was filled with astonishment.

New species have appeared very slowly, one after another, both on the land and in the waters.

This gradual increase in number of the species of a group is strictly conformable with the theory, for the species of the same genus, and the genera of the same family, can increase only slowly and progressively; the process of modification and the production of a number of allied forms necessarily being a slow and gradual process, one species first giving rise to two or three varieties, these being slowly converted into species, which in their turn produce by equally slow steps other varieties, and species, and so on, like the branching of a great tree from a single stem, till the group becomes large.

Grazers

6 MILLION YEARS AGO

ASTROHIPPUS   PLIOHIPPUS

CALIHIPPUS

PARAHI

Browsers

Browsers

40 MILLION YEARS AGO

MESOHIPPUS

MIOHIPPUS

EPIHIPPUS

Browsers

HAPLOHIPPUS

OROHIPPUS

PROPALAEOT

55 MILLION YEARS AGO

PACHYNOLOPHUS

PROTOROHIPPUS

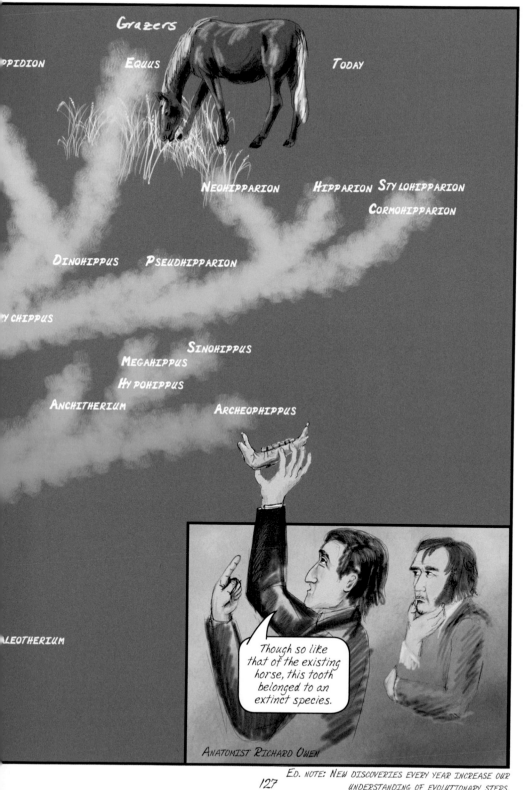

ED. NOTE: NEW DISCOVERIES EVERY YEAR INCREASE OUR
UNDERSTANDING OF EVOLUTIONARY STEPS.

Whether such variations or individual differences as may arise will be accumulated through natural selection in a greater or less degree,

Before 1850

CHANGE IN PEPPERED MOTH COLOUR PROPORTIONS

—1850

PRIOR TO 1850, LICHEN COVERED TREES IN ENGLAND.

PEPPERED MOTH
(BISTON BETULARIA—MORPHA TYPICA)

POLLUTION FROM THE INDUSTRIAL REVOLUTION DARKENED TREES AND KILLED LIGHT LICHEN.

PEPPERED MOTH
(BISTON BETULARIA—MORPHA CARBONARIA)

thus causing a greater or less amount of permanent modification, will depend on many complex contingencies,

on the variations being of a beneficial nature, on the freedom of intercrossing, on the slowly changing physical conditions of the country, on the immigration of new colonists, and on the nature of the other inhabitants with which the varying species come into competition.

ED. NOTE: THE LIGHT VARIATION HAS AGAIN BECOME MORE COMMON AS POLLUTION HAS DECREASED.

When advanced up to any given point, there is no necessity, on the theory of natural selection, for their further continued progress; though they will, during each successive age, have to be slightly modified, so as to hold their places in relation to slight changes in their conditions.

Any form which did not become in some degree modified and improved would be liable to extermination.

The extinction of old forms and the production of new and improved forms are intimately connected together. The old notion of all the inhabitants of the earth having been swept away by catastrophes at successive periods is very generally given up.

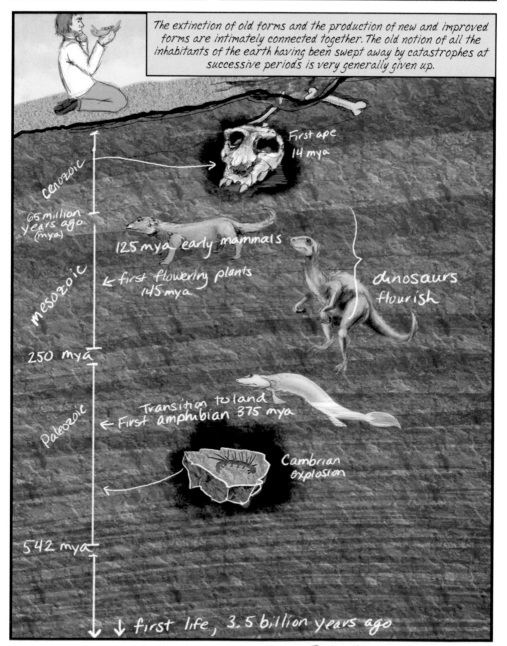

First ape 14 mya

Cenozoic

65 million years ago (mya)

Mesozoic

125 mya early mammals

← first flowering plants 145 mya

dinosaurs flourish

250 mya

Paleozoic

Transition to land
← First amphibian 375 mya

Cambrian explosion

542 mya

↓ first life, 3.5 billion years ago

ED NOTE: NOT TO SCALE, NOR COMPREHENSIVE

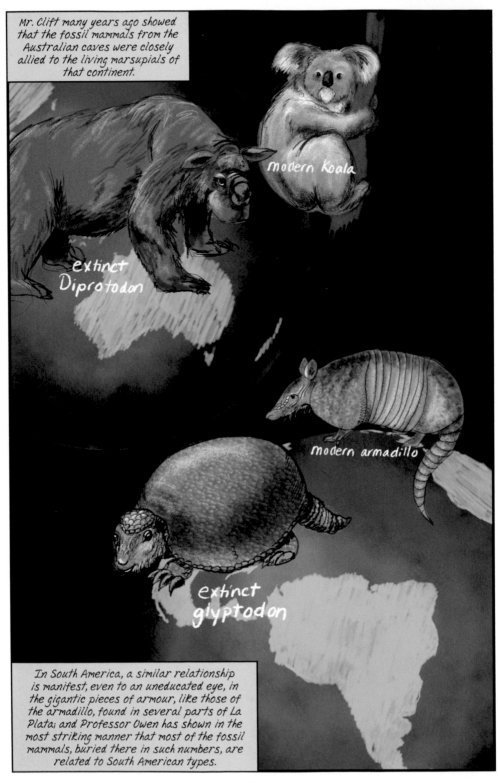

Mr. Clift many years ago showed that the fossil mammals from the Australian caves were closely allied to the living marsupials of that continent.

modern koala

extinct Diprotodon

modern armadillo

extinct glyptodon

In South America, a similar relationship is manifest, even to an uneducated eye, in the gigantic pieces of armour, like those of the armadillo, found in several parts of La Plata; and Professor Owen has shown in the most striking manner that most of the fossil mammals, buried there in such numbers, are related to South American types.

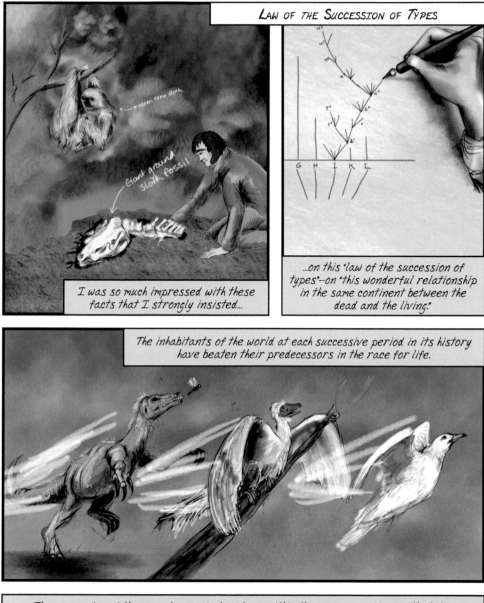

modern tree sloth

Giant ground Sloth fossil

I was so much impressed with these facts that I strongly insisted...

...on this "law of the succession of types"—on "this wonderful relationship in the same continent between the dead and the living."

The inhabitants of the world at each successive period in its history have beaten their predecessors in the race for life.

The succession of the same types of structure within the same areas during the later geological periods ceases to be mysterious, and is intelligible on the principle of inheritance.

Small tree finch
(Camarhynchus parvulus)
insect eater

probing bill

Green Warbler Finch
(Certhidea olivacea)
insect eater

Medium Ground Finch
(Geospiza fortis)
seed eater

seed eater
Large Ground Finch
(Geospiza magnirostris)

CHAPTERS 12 & 13

GEOGRAPHICAL DISTRIBUTION

IN WHICH WE INVESTIGATE THE PLACES WHERE WE COME ACROSS DIFFERENT
SPECIES OF ORGANISMS. WE FIND THE MANNER OF THE DISTRIBUTION TO BE
EXPLAINABLE AS PATTERNS OF MIGRATION AWAY FROM POINTS OF ORIGIN, NOT BY
SPECIES BEING INDIVIDUALLY CREATED IN THE LANDS WHERE WE NOW FIND THEM.

One of the most fundamental divisions in geographical distribution is that between the New and Old Worlds,

yet if we travel over the vast American continent, from the central parts of the United States to its extreme southern point, we meet with the most diversified conditions.

SPOTTED OWL
(STRIX OCCIDENTALIS)

BLUE POISON DART FROG
(DENDROBATES AZUREUS)

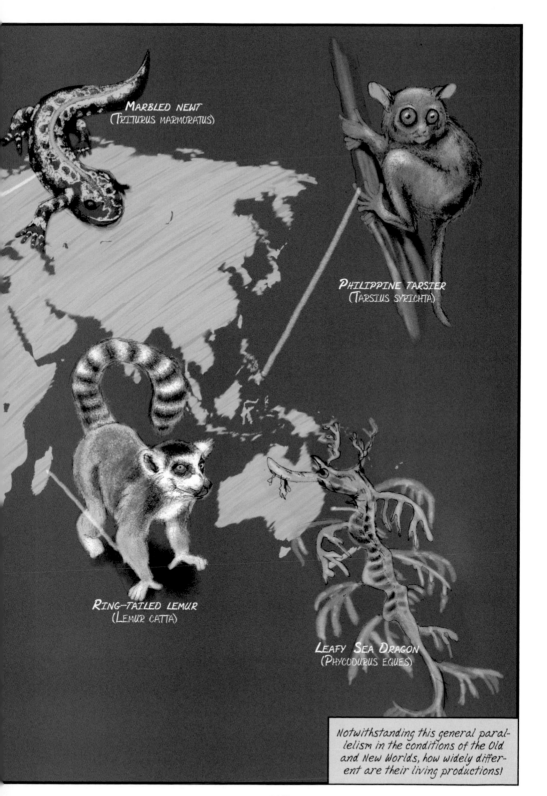

MARBLED NEWT
(TRITURUS MARMORATUS)

PHILIPPINE TARSIER
(TARSIUS SYRICHTA)

RING-TAILED LEMUR
(LEMUR CATTA)

LEAFY SEA DRAGON
(PHYCODURUS EQUES)

Notwithstanding this general paral-
lelism in the conditions of the Old
and New Worlds, how widely different are their living productions!

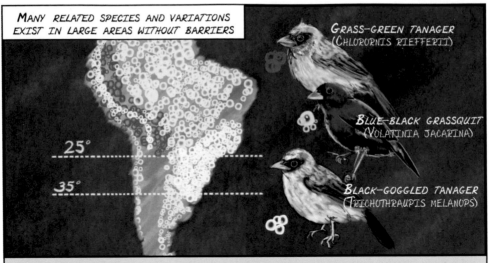

MANY RELATED SPECIES AND VARIATIONS EXIST IN LARGE AREAS WITHOUT BARRIERS

GRASS-GREEN TANAGER
(CHLOROPHONUS RIEFFERTI)

BLUE-BLACK GRASSQUIT
(VOLATINIA JACARINA)

BLACK-GOGGLED TANAGER
(TRICHOTHRAUPIS MELANOPS)

25°

35°

We may compare the productions of South America south of latitude 35° with those north of 25°, which consequently are separated by a space of ten degrees of latitude, and are exposed to considerably different conditions,

WHEN OBSTACLES TO MIGRATION EXIST, OFTEN UNRELATED SPECIES FILL SIMILAR NICHES

JAGUAR
(PANTHERA ONCA)

LION
(PANTHERA LEO)

MARSUPIAL LION
(THYLACOLEO CARNIFEX)

35°

35°

35°

yet they are incomparably more closely related to each other than they are to the productions of Australia or Africa under nearly the same climate.

Barriers of any kind, or obstacles to free migration, are related in a close and important manner to the differences between the productions of various regions. We see this in the great differences in nearly all the terrestrial productions of the New and Old Worlds.

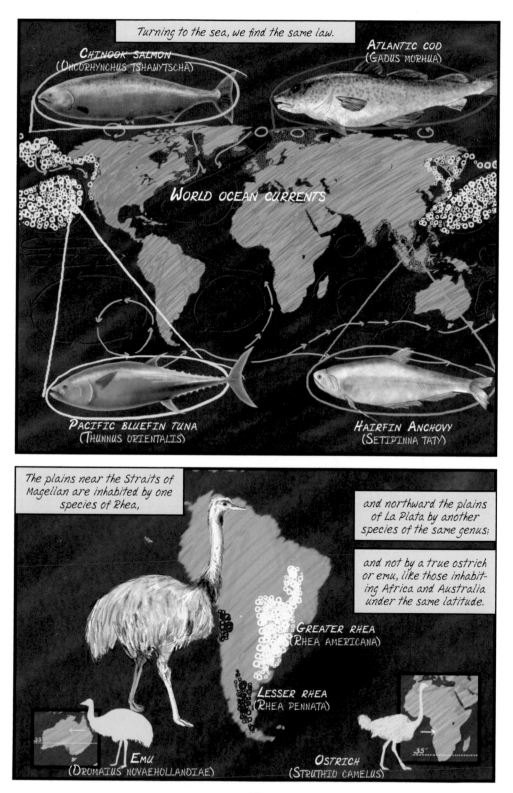

Turning to the sea, we find the same law.

CHINOOK SALMON
(ONCORHYNCHUS TSHAWYTSCHA)

ATLANTIC COD
(GADUS MORHUA)

WORLD OCEAN CURRENTS

PACIFIC BLUEFIN TUNA
(THUNNUS ORIENTALIS)

HAIRFIN ANCHOVY
(SETIPINNA TATY)

The plains near the Straits of Magellan are inhabited by one species of Rhea,

and northward the plains of La Plata by another species of the same genus;

and not by a true ostrich or emu, like those inhabiting Africa and Australia under the same latitude.

GREATER RHEA
(RHEA AMERICANA)

LESSER RHEA
(RHEA PENNATA)

EMU
(DROMAIUS NOVAEHOLLANDIAE)

OSTRICH
(STRUTHIO CAMELUS)

On these same plains of La Plata we see the agouti and [viscacha], animals having nearly the same habits as our hares and rabbits, and belonging to the same order of rodents, but they plainly display an [South] American type of structure.

35°

Jack rabbit

Viscacha

Capybara

Beaver

We look to the waters, and we do not find the beaver or musk-rat, but the coypu and capybara, rodents of the South American type.

If we look to the islands off the American shore, however much they may differ in geological structure, the inhabitants are essentially American, though they may be all peculiar species.

We see in these facts some deep organic bond, throughout space and time, over the same areas of land and water, independently of physical conditions.

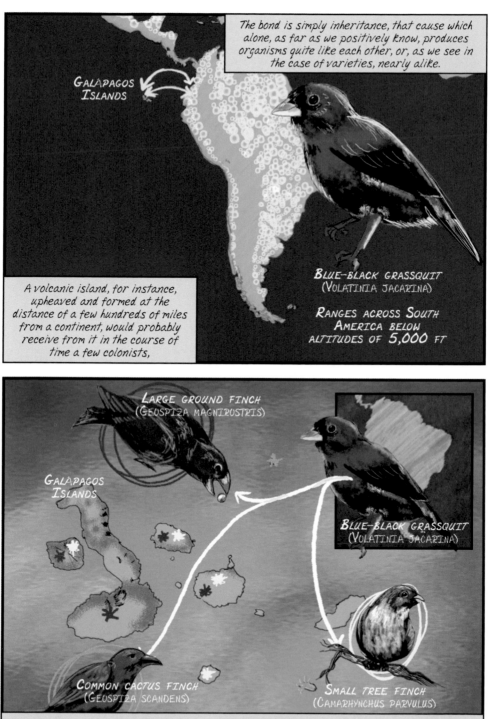

The bond is simply inheritance, that cause which alone, as far as we positively know, produces organisms quite like each other, or, as we see in the case of varieties, nearly alike.

GALÁPAGOS ISLANDS

A volcanic island, for instance, upheaved and formed at the distance of a few hundreds of miles from a continent, would probably receive from it in the course of time a few colonists,

BLUE-BLACK GRASSQUIT
(VOLATINIA JACARINA)

RANGES ACROSS SOUTH AMERICA BELOW ALTITUDES OF 5,000 FT

LARGE GROUND FINCH
(GEOSPIZA MAGNIROSTRIS)

GALÁPAGOS ISLANDS

BLUE-BLACK GRASSQUIT
(VOLATINIA JACARINA)

COMMON CACTUS FINCH
(GEOSPIZA SCANDENS)

SMALL TREE FINCH
(CAMARHYNCHUS PARVULUS)

and their descendants, though modified, would still be related by inheritance to the inhabitants of that continent. In their new homes they will be exposed to new conditions, and will frequently undergo further modification and improvement; and thus they will become still further victorious, and will produce groups of modified descendants.

ED. NOTE: SOME SCIENTISTS HAVE THEORIZED VOLATINIA JACARINA IS THE ANCESTOR OF THE GALÁPAGOS FINCHES, BUT THIS IS DEBATED.

MEANS OF MIGRATION

Thus the high importance of barriers comes into play by checking migration.

To: J. Henslow, 28 March 1837

...At some future time I shall want to know the number of species of plants at Galapagos and Keeling, and at the latter whether seeds could probably endure floating on salt water...

Hence it seems to me, as it has to many other naturalists, that the view of each species having been produced in one area alone, and having subsequently migrated from that area as far as its powers of migration and subsistence under past and present conditions permitted, is the most probable.

Until I tried, with Mr. Berkeley's aid, a few experiments, it was not even known how far seeds could resist the injurious action of sea-water.

To my surprise I found that out of 87 kinds,

64 germinated after an immersion of 28 days, and a few survived an immersion of 137 days.

The average rate of the several Atlantic currents is 33 miles per diem (some currents running at the rate of 60 miles per diem).

On this average, the seeds of 14,100 plants belonging to one country might be floated across 924 miles of sea to another country, and when stranded, if blown by an inland gale to a favorable spot, would germinate.

Seeds may be occasionally transported in another manner.

Living birds can hardly fail to be highly effective agents in the transportation of seeds.

In the course of two months, I picked up in my garden 12 kinds of seeds, out of the excrement of small birds, and these seemed perfect, and some of them, which were tried, germinated.

Although the beaks and feet of birds are generally clean, earth sometimes adheres to them.

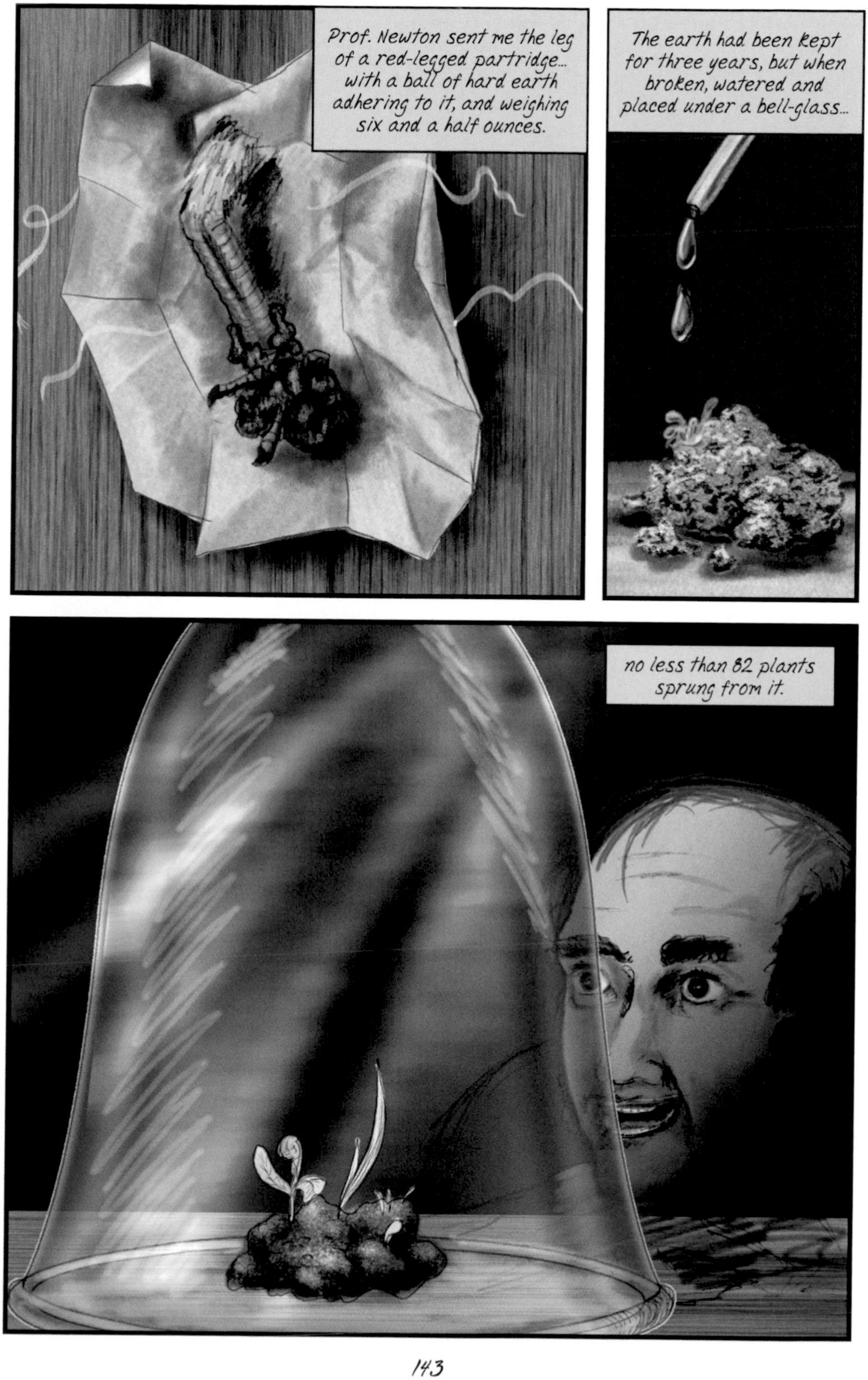
Prof. Newton sent me the leg of a red-legged partridge... with a ball of hard earth adhering to it, and weighing six and a half ounces.
The earth had been kept for three years, but when broken, watered and placed under a bell-glass...
no less than 82 plants sprung from it.

When first collecting in the fresh waters of Brazil, I well remember feeling much surprise at the similarity of the fresh-water insects, shells, &c., and at the dissimilarity of the surrounding terrestrial beings, compared with those of Britain.

As lakes and river systems are separated from each other by barriers of land, it might have been thought that fresh-water productions would not have ranged widely within the same country,

NEW ZEALAND

and as the sea is apparently a still more formidable barrier, that they would never have extended to distant countries.

But Dr. Gunther has lately shown that the Galaxias attenuatus inhabits Tasmania, New Zealand, the Falkland Islands, and the mainland of South America. It was formerly believed that the same fresh-water species never existed on two continents distant from each other.

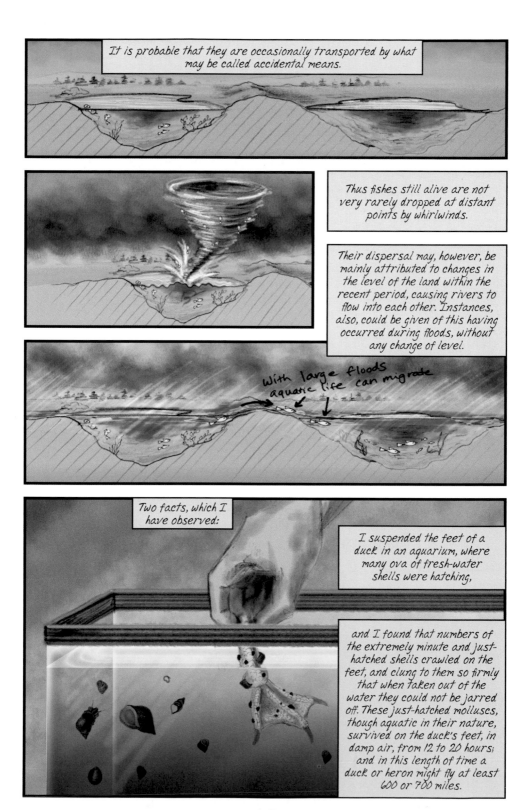

It is probable that they are occasionally transported by what may be called accidental means.

Thus fishes still alive are not very rarely dropped at distant points by whirlwinds.

Their dispersal may, however, be mainly attributed to changes in the level of the land within the recent period, causing rivers to flow into each other. Instances, also, could be given of this having occurred during floods, without any change of level.

With large floods aquatic life can migrate

Two facts, which I have observed:

I suspended the feet of a duck in an aquarium, where many ova of fresh-water shells were hatching,

and I found that numbers of the extremely minute and just-hatched shells crawled on the feet, and clung to them so firmly that when taken out of the water they could not be jarred off. These just-hatched molluscs, though aquatic in their nature, survived on the duck's feet, in damp air, from 12 to 20 hours; and in this length of time a duck or heron might fly at least 600 or 700 miles.

145

With respect to the absence of whole orders of animals on oceanic islands,

BARON JEAN BAPTISTE GENEVIÈVE MARCELLIN BORY DE SAINT-VINCENT, FRENCH NATURALIST

RÉUNION ISLAND

Baron St. Vincent long ago remarked that batrachians (frogs, toads, newts) are never found on any of the many islands with which the great oceans are studded.

I have taken pains to verify this assertion, and have found it true, with the exception of New Zealand, New Caledonia, the Andaman Islands, and perhaps the Solomon Islands and the Seychelles.

GALÁPAGOS ISLANDS

This general absence of frogs, toads, and newts on so many true oceanic islands cannot be accounted for by their physical conditions: indeed it seems that islands are peculiarly fitted for these animals,

for frogs have been introduced into Madeira, the Azores, and Mauritius, and have multiplied so as to become a nuisance.

But as these animals and their spawn are immediately killed (with the exception, as far as known, of one Indian species) by sea-water, there would be great difficulty in their transportal across the sea, and therefore we can see why they do not exist on strictly oceanic islands.

HEALTHY FROG EGG IN FRESHWATER

FROG EGG IN SALTWATER

FROG EGG OUT OF WATER

But why, on the theory of creation, they should not have been created there, it would be very difficult to explain.

Mammals offer another and similar case.

I have carefully searched the oldest voyages, and have not found a single instance, free from doubt, of a terrestrial mammal (excluding domesticated animals kept by the natives) inhabiting an island situated above 300 miles from a continent or great continental island.

Although terrestrial mammals do not occur on oceanic islands,

TAPIR

aerial mammals do occur on almost every island.

Why, it may be asked, has the supposed creative force produced bats and no other mammals on remote islands?

New Zealand possesses two bats found nowhere else in the world: Norfolk Island, the Viti Archipelago, the Bonin Islands, the Caroline and Marianne Archipelagoes, and Mauritius, all possess their peculiar bats.

Viti

Norfolk

Bonin

Caroline

On my view this question can easily be answered:

for no terrestrial mammal can be transported across a wide space of sea,

but bats can fly across.

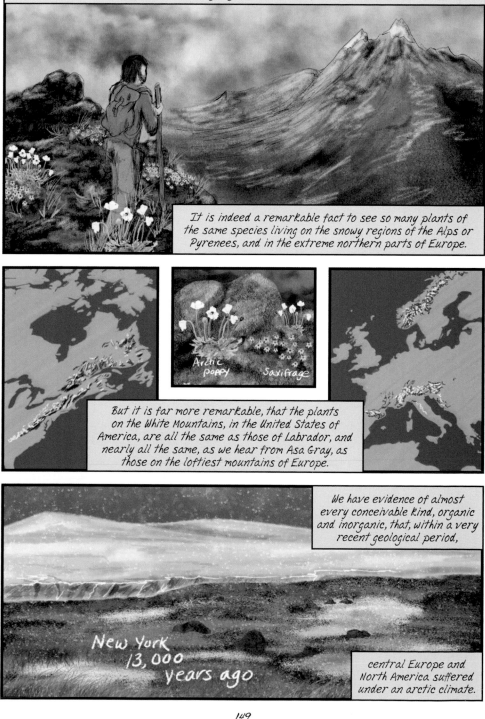

The identity of many plants and animals, on mountain summits, separated from each other by hundreds of miles of lowlands, where Alpine species could not possibly exist, is one of the most striking cases known of the same species living at distant points, without the apparent possibility of their having migrated from one point to the other.

It is indeed a remarkable fact to see so many plants of the same species living on the snowy regions of the Alps or Pyrenees, and in the extreme northern parts of Europe.

Arctic poppy

Saxifrage

But it is far more remarkable, that the plants on the White Mountains, in the United States of America, are all the same as those of Labrador, and nearly all the same, as we hear from Asa Gray, as those on the loftiest mountains of Europe.

We have evidence of almost every conceivable kind, organic and inorganic, that, within a very recent geological period,

New York 13,000 years ago

central Europe and North America suffered under an arctic climate.

135,000 YEARS AGO — *THE CLIMATE WAS MUCH LIKE OURS TODAY*

As the cold came on, and as each more southern zone became fitted for the inhabitants of the north, these would take the places of the former inhabitants of the temperate regions.

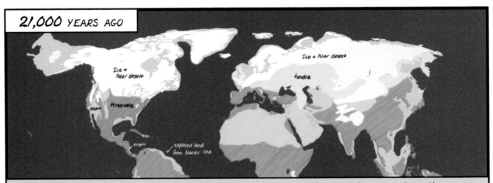

21,000 YEARS AGO

The latter, at the same time, would travel further and further southward, unless they were stopped by barriers, in which case they would perish. The mountains would become covered with snow and ice, and their former Alpine inhabitants would descend to the plains. By the time that the cold had reached its maximum, we should have an arctic fauna and flora, covering the central parts of Europe, as far south as the Alps and Pyrenees, and even stretching into Spain.

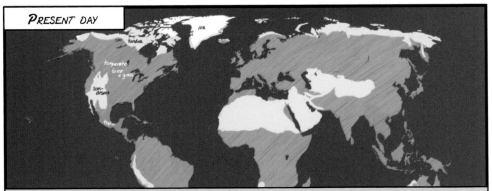

PRESENT DAY

And as the snow melted from the bases of the mountains, the arctic forms would seize on the cleared and thawed ground, always ascending, as the warmth increased and the snow still further disappeared, higher and higher, whilst their brethren were pursuing their northern journey. Hence, when the warmth had fully returned, the same species, which had lately lived together on the European and North American lowlands, would again be found in the arctic regions of the Old and New Worlds, and on many isolated mountain summits far distant from each other.

CHAPTER 14

MUTUAL AFFINITIES OF ORGANIC BEINGS: MORPHOLOGY: EMBRYOLOGY: RUDIMENTARY ORGANS

HERE I WOULD LIKE TO DIRECT YOUR ATTENTION TO DIVERSE FIELDS OF STUDY, ALL OF WHICH BEAR THE PROOF AND HISTORY OF THE COMMON ANCESTRY OF ALL ORGANISMS AND THE INTEGRAL PART NATURAL SELECTION PLAYS IN CREATING NEW BRANCHES ON THE TREE OF LIFE.

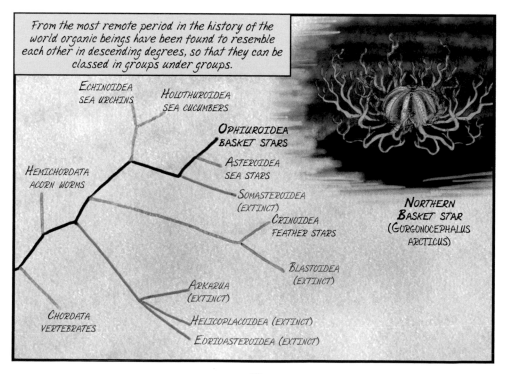

From the most remote period in the history of the world organic beings have been found to resemble each other in descending degrees, so that they can be classed in groups under groups.

ECHINOIDEA
SEA URCHINS

HOLOTHUROIDEA
SEA CUCUMBERS

OPHIUROIDEA
BASKET STARS

ASTEROIDEA
SEA STARS

SOMASTEROIDEA
(EXTINCT)

HEMICHORDATA
ACORN WORMS

CRINOIDEA
FEATHER STARS

BLASTOIDEA
(EXTINCT)

ARKARUA
(EXTINCT)

CHORDATA
VERTEBRATES

HELICOPLACOIDEA (EXTINCT)

EDRIOASTEROIDEA (EXTINCT)

NORTHERN
BASKET STAR
(GORGONOCEPHALUS
ARCTICUS)

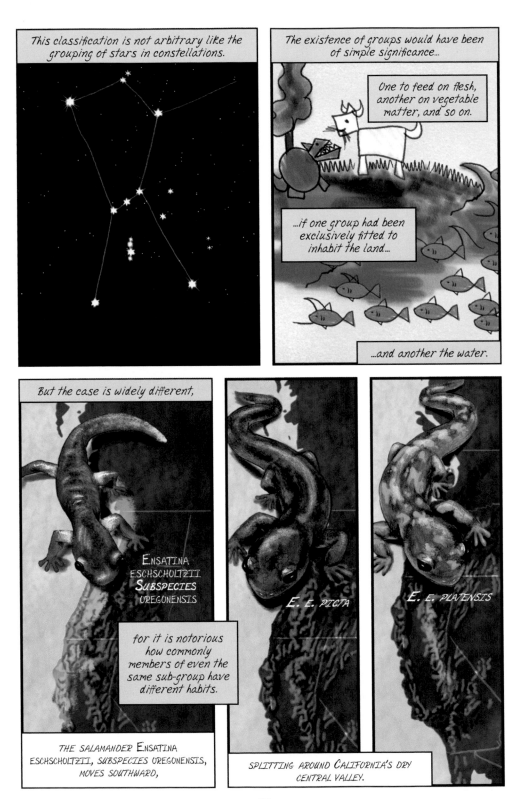

This classification is not arbitrary like the grouping of stars in constellations.

The existence of groups would have been of simple significance...

One to feed on flesh, another on vegetable matter, and so on.

...if one group had been exclusively fitted to inhabit the land...

...and another the water.

But the case is widely different,

ENSATINA ESCHSCHOLTZII SUBSPECIES OREGONENSIS

for it is notorious how commonly members of even the same sub-group have different habits.

E. E. PICTA

E. E. PLATENSIS

THE SALAMANDER ENSATINA ESCHSCHOLTZII, SUBSPECIES OREGONENSIS, MOVES SOUTHWARD,

SPLITTING AROUND CALIFORNIA'S DRY CENTRAL VALLEY.

E. E. XANTHOPTICA

E. E. ESCHSCHOLTZII

E. E. KLAUBERI

E. E. CROCEATER

INCIPIENT SPECIATION

The varieties, or incipient species, thus produced, ultimately become converted into new and distinct species; and these, on the principle of inheritance, tend to produce other new and dominant species.... They constantly tend to diverge in character.

AFTER BEING ISOLATED BY MOUNTAIN RANGES, SOME SPECIES OF ENSATINA CAN NO LONGER MATE WITH EACH OTHER IN NATURE, EVEN WHERE THEIR RANGES MEET.

ED. NOTE: FROM THE PIONEERING SPECIATION WORK BY DAVID B. WAKE, UNIVERSITY OF CALIFORNIA, BERKELEY.

The ingenuity and utility of this system [of groups] are indisputable.

But many naturalists think that something more is meant by the Natural System; they believe that it reveals the plan of the Creator; that unless it be specified whether order in time or space, or both, or what else is meant by the plan of the Creator, it seems to me that nothing is thus added to our knowledge.

African monarch
(Danaus chrysippus)

Mimic butterfly
(Papilio dardanus form lamborni)

Domesticated dog
(Canis lupus familiaris)

Extinct
Tasmanian wolf
(Thylacine cynocephalus)

The Natural System is founded on descent with modification; that the characters which naturalists consider as showing true affinity between any two or more species, are those which have been inherited from a common parent, all true classification being genealogical; that community of descent is the hidden bond which naturalists have been unconsciously seeking, and not some unknown plan of creation.

The principle formerly alluded to under the term of analogical variation has probably in these cases often come into play; that is, the members of the same class, although only distantly allied, have inherited so much in common in their constitution, that they are apt to vary under similar exciting causes in a similar manner; and this would obviously aid in the acquirement through natural selection of parts or organs, strikingly like each other, independently of their direct inheritance from a common progenitor.

ANALOGICAL RESEMBLANCES

4 pre-molars

2 molars

Dog Skull

Tasmanian wolf skull

3 pre-molars

4 molars

A good instance is afforded by the close resemblance of the jaws of the dog and Tasmanian wolf or Thylacinus—animals which are widely sundered in the natural system. But this resemblance is confined to general appearance, as in the prominence of the canines, and in the cutting shape of the molar teeth.

For the teeth really differ much: thus the dog has on each side of the upper jaw four pre-molars and only two molars; whilst the Thylacinus has three pre-molars and four molars.

155

Certain butterflies imitate, as first described by Mr. Bates, other and quite distinct species. When the mockers and the mocked are caught and compared, they are found to be very different in essential structure.

INEDIBLE

MIMIC

PAPILIO POLYMNESTOR

P. MEMNON POLYMNESTOROIDES

AMAURIS NIAVIUS

P. DARDANUS HIPPOCOON

AMAURIS ECHERIA

P. D. CENEA

DANAUS CHRYSIPPUS

P. D. LAMBORNI

The mockers and mocked always inhabit the same region; we never find an imitator living remote from the form which it imitates.

AFRICAN PARADISE FLYCATCHER (TERPSIPHONE VIRIDIS)

But why, it may be asked, are certain forms treated as the mimicked and others as the mimickers?

DANAUS CHRYSIPPUS

Why, to the perplexity of naturalists, has nature condescended to the tricks of the stage?

P. D. LAMBORNI

The mocked forms, which always abound in numbers, must habitually escape destruction to a large extent, otherwise they could not exist in such swarms;

and a large amount of evidence has now been collected, showing that they are distasteful to birds and other insect-devouring animals.

P. D. LAMBORNI

Professor Häckel...has recently brought his great knowledge and abilities to bear on what he calls phylogeny, or the lines of descent of all organic beings. In drawing up the several series he trusts chiefly to embryological characters, but receives aid from homologous and rudimentary organs, as well as from the successive periods at which the various forms of life are believed to have first appeared in our geological formations....

We have seen that the members of the same class, independently of their habits of life, resemble each other in the general plan of their organisation. This resemblance is often expressed by the term "unity of type"; or by saying that the several parts and organs in the different species of the class are homologous.... This is one of the most interesting departments of natural history, and may almost be said to be its very soul.

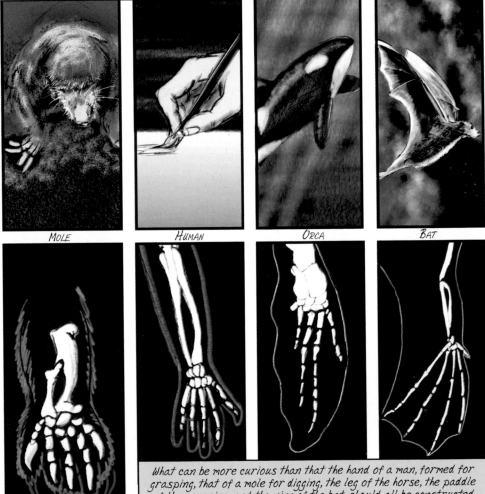

MOLE　　　HUMAN　　　ORCA　　　BAT

What can be more curious than that the hand of a man, formed for grasping, that of a mole for digging, the leg of the horse, the paddle of the porpoise, and the wing of the bat, should all be constructed on the same pattern, and should include similar bones, in the same relative positions?...

Geoffroy St. Hilaire has strongly insisted on the high importance of relative position or connexion in homologous parts; they may differ to almost any extent in form and size, and yet remain connected together in the same invariable order. We never find, for instance, the bones of the arm and fore-arm, or of the thigh and leg, transposed....

DINOSAUR

MANATEE

FROG

GORILLA

We see the same great law in the construction of the mouths of insects: what can be more different than the immensely long spiral proboscis of a sphinx-moth, the curious folded one of a bee or bug, and the great jaws of a beetle? Yet all these organs, serving for such widely different purposes, are formed by infinitely numerous modifications of an upper lip, mandibles, and two pairs of maxillae.

WASP

MOTH

FLY

Why should the brain be enclosed in a box composed of such numerous and such extraordinarily shaped pieces of bone, apparently representing vertebrae?...

Why should similar bones have been created to form the wing and the leg of a bat, used as they are for such totally different purposes, namely flying and walking?...

Why should the sepals, petals, stamens, and pistils, in each flower, though fitted for such distinct purposes, be all constructed on the same pattern?

On the ordinary view of the independent creation of each being, we can only say that so it is; that it has pleased the Creator to construct all the animals and plants in each great class on a uniform plan; but this is not a scientific explanation.

This is one of the most important subjects in the whole round of natural history. It is...an astonishing fact that a delicate branching coralline, studded with polypi and attached to a submarine rock, should produce, first by budding and then by transverse division, a host of huge floating jelly-fishes; and that these should produce eggs, from which are hatched swimming animalcules, which attach themselves to rocks and become developed into branching corallines; and so on in an endless cycle....

It has already been stated that various parts in the same individual which are exactly alike during an early embryonic period, become widely different and serve for widely different purposes in the adult state.

So again it has been shown that generally the embryos of the most distinct species belonging to the same class are closely similar, but become, when fully developed, widely dissimilar.

A better proof...cannot be given than the statement of Von Baer that "the embryos of mammalia, of birds, lizards, and snakes, probably also of chelonia, are in their earliest states exceedingly like one another, both as a whole and in the mode of development of their parts....

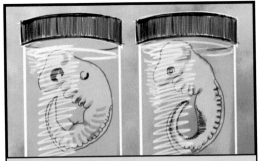

In my possession are two little embryos in spirit.... They may be lizards or small birds, or very young mammalia, so complete is the similarity in the mode of formation of the head and trunk in these animals...."

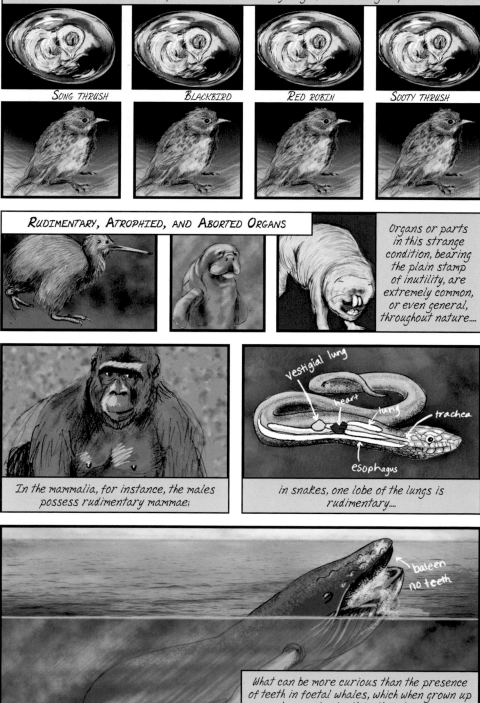

A trace of the law of embryonic resemblance occasionally lasts till a rather late age: thus birds of the same genus, and of allied genera, often resemble each other in their immature plumage; as we see in the spotted feathers in the young of the thrush group.

SONG THRUSH

BLACKBIRD

RED ROBIN

SOOTY THRUSH

RUDIMENTARY, ATROPHIED, AND ABORTED ORGANS

Organs or parts in this strange condition, bearing the plain stamp of inutility, are extremely common, or even general, throughout nature....

In the mammalia, for instance, the males possess rudimentary mammae;

vestigial lung

heart

lung

trachea

esophagus

in snakes, one lobe of the lungs is rudimentary....

baleen
no teeth

What can be more curious than the presence of teeth in foetal whales, which when grown up have not a tooth in their heads?...

161

Rudimentary organs sometimes retain their potentiality: this occasionally occurs with the mammae of male mammals, which have been known to become well developed and to secrete milk.

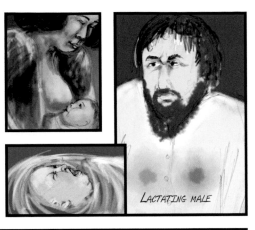

LACTATING MALE

The wing of the penguin is of high service, acting as a fin; it may, therefore, represent the nascent state of the wing;...it is more probably a reduced organ, modified for a new function;

the wing of the Apteryx, on the other hand, is quite useless, and is truly rudimentary.

APTERYX

In works on natural history, rudimentary organs are generally said to have been created "for the sake of symmetry," or in order "to complete the scheme of nature." But this is not an explanation, merely a re-statement of the fact. Nor is it consistent with itself: thus the boa-constrictor has rudiments of hind limbs and of a pelvis, and if it be said that these bones have been retained "to complete the scheme of nature," why, as Professor Weismann asks, have they not been retained by other snakes, which do not possess even a vestige of these same bones? What would be thought of an astronomer who maintained that the satellites revolve in elliptic courses round their planets "for the sake of symmetry", because the planets thus revolve round the sun?

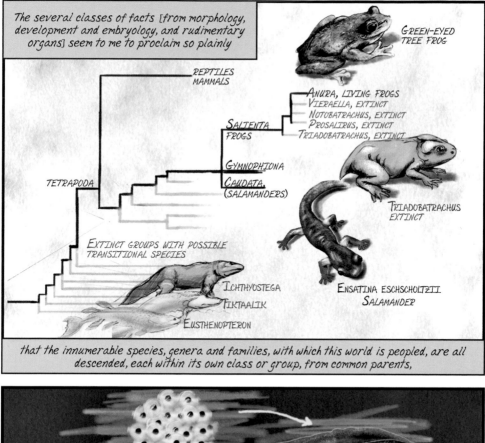

The several classes of facts [from morphology, development and embryology, and rudimentary organs] seem to me to proclaim so plainly

GREEN-EYED TREE FROG

REPTILES
MAMMALS

ANURA, LIVING FROGS
VIERAELLA, EXTINCT
NOTOBATRACHUS, EXTINCT
PROSALIRUS, EXTINCT
TRIADOBATRACHUS, EXTINCT

SALIENTA
FROGS

GYMNOPHIONA

CAUDATA,
(SALAMANDERS)

TETRAPODA

TRIADOBATRACHUS
EXTINCT

EXTINCT GROUPS WITH POSSIBLE
TRANSITIONAL SPECIES

ICHTHYOSTEGA
TIKTAALIK
EUSTHENOPTERON

ENSATINA ESCHSCHOLTZII
SALAMANDER

that the innumerable species, genera and families, with which this world is peopled, are all descended, each within its own class or group, from common parents,

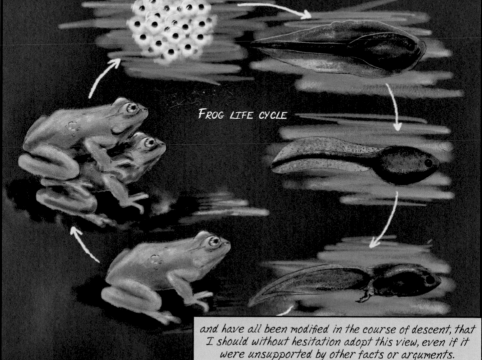

FROG LIFE CYCLE

and have all been modified in the course of descent, that I should without hesitation adopt this view, even if it were unsupported by other facts or arguments.

CHAPTER 15

RECAPITULATION AND CONCLUSION

IN WHICH, AFTER BRINGING AS MANY OF MY OBSERVATIONS TO BEAR ON THE
SUBJECT OF EVOLUTION AS I CAN, I END MY ONE LONG ARGUMENT FOR DESCENT
WITH MODIFICATION AND NATURAL SELECTION AS ITS DRIVING FORCE.

It is interesting to contemplate a tangled
bank, clothed with many plants of many kinds,
with birds singing on the bushes, with various
insects flitting about, and with worms crawling
through the damp earth,

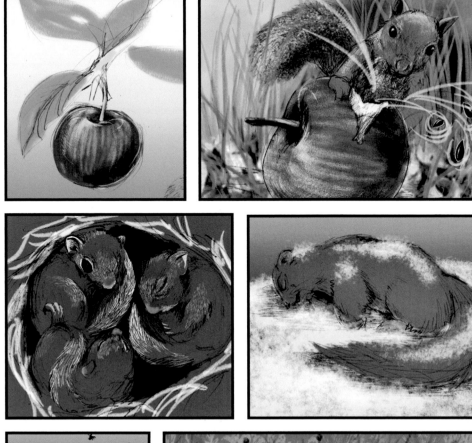

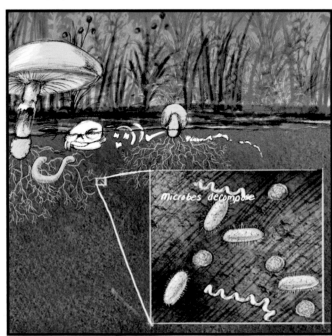

and to reflect that these elaborately constructed forms, so different from each other, and dependent upon each other in so complex a manner, have all been produced by laws acting around us.

microbes decompose

These laws, taken in the largest sense, being Growth with Reproduction; Inheritance which is almost implied by reproduction; Variability from the indirect and direct action of the conditions of life, and from use and disuse: a Ratio of Increase so high as to lead to a Struggle for Life, and as a consequence to Natural Selection, entailing Divergence of Character and the Extinction of less-improved forms.

Thus, from the war of nature, from famine and death, the most exalted object which we are capable of conceiving, namely, the production of the higher animals, directly follows.

There is grandeur in this view of life, with its several powers, having been originally breathed by the Creator into a few forms or into one;

and that, whilst this planet has gone cycling on according to the fixed law of gravity, from so simple a beginning endless forms most beautiful and most wonderful have been, and are being, evolved.

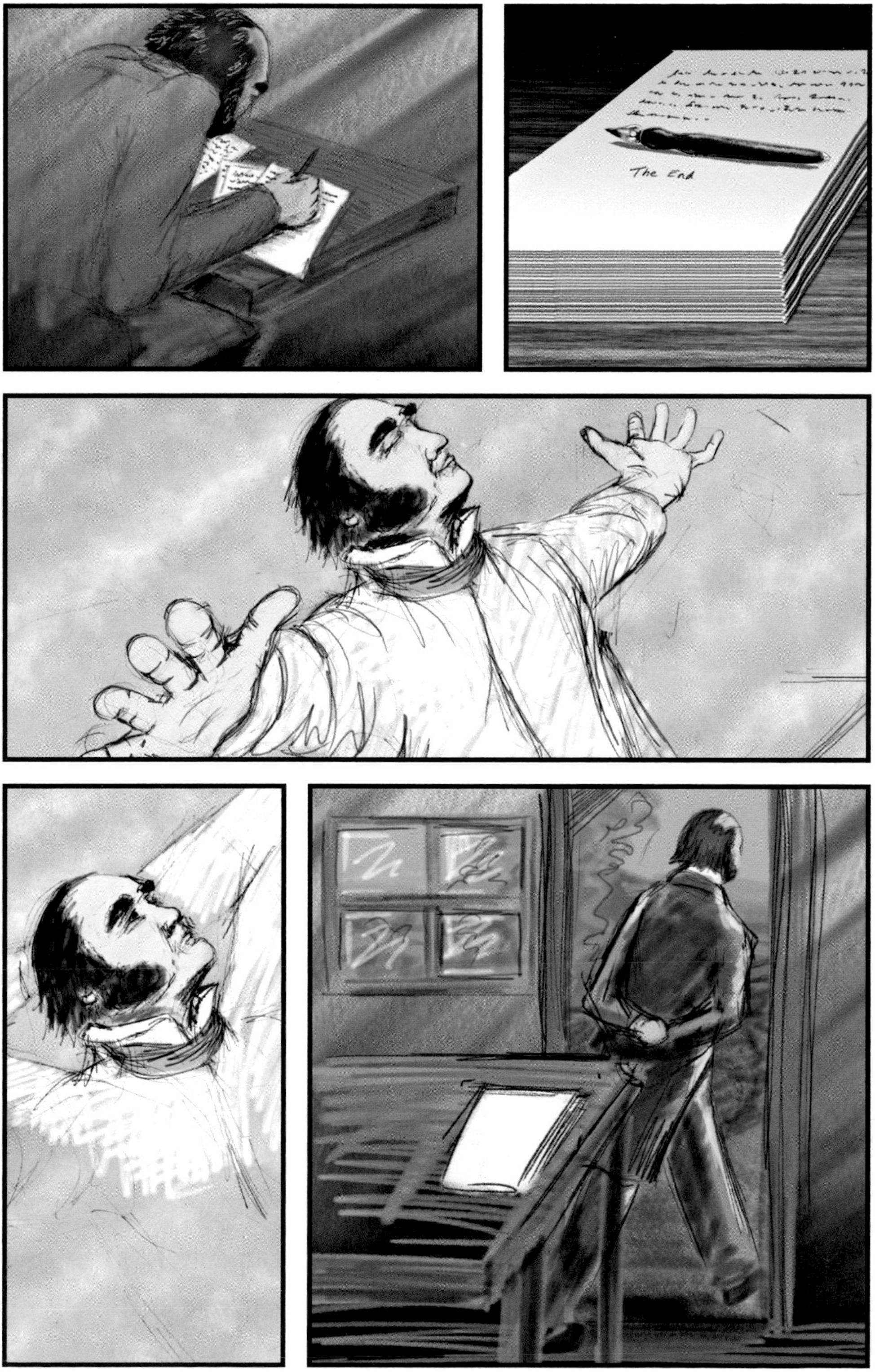
The End

Part 3

Afterword

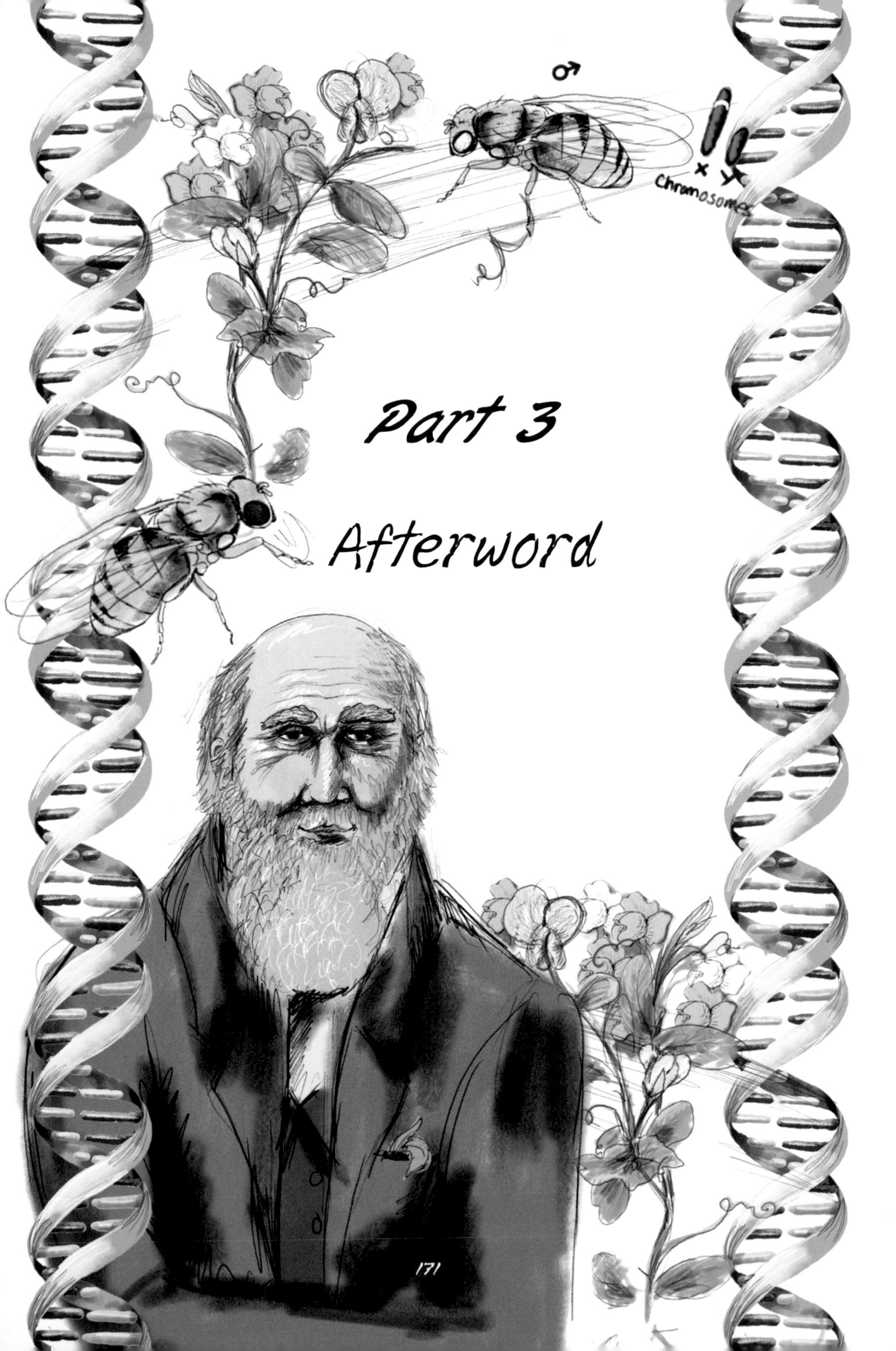
♂
X Y
Chromosomes

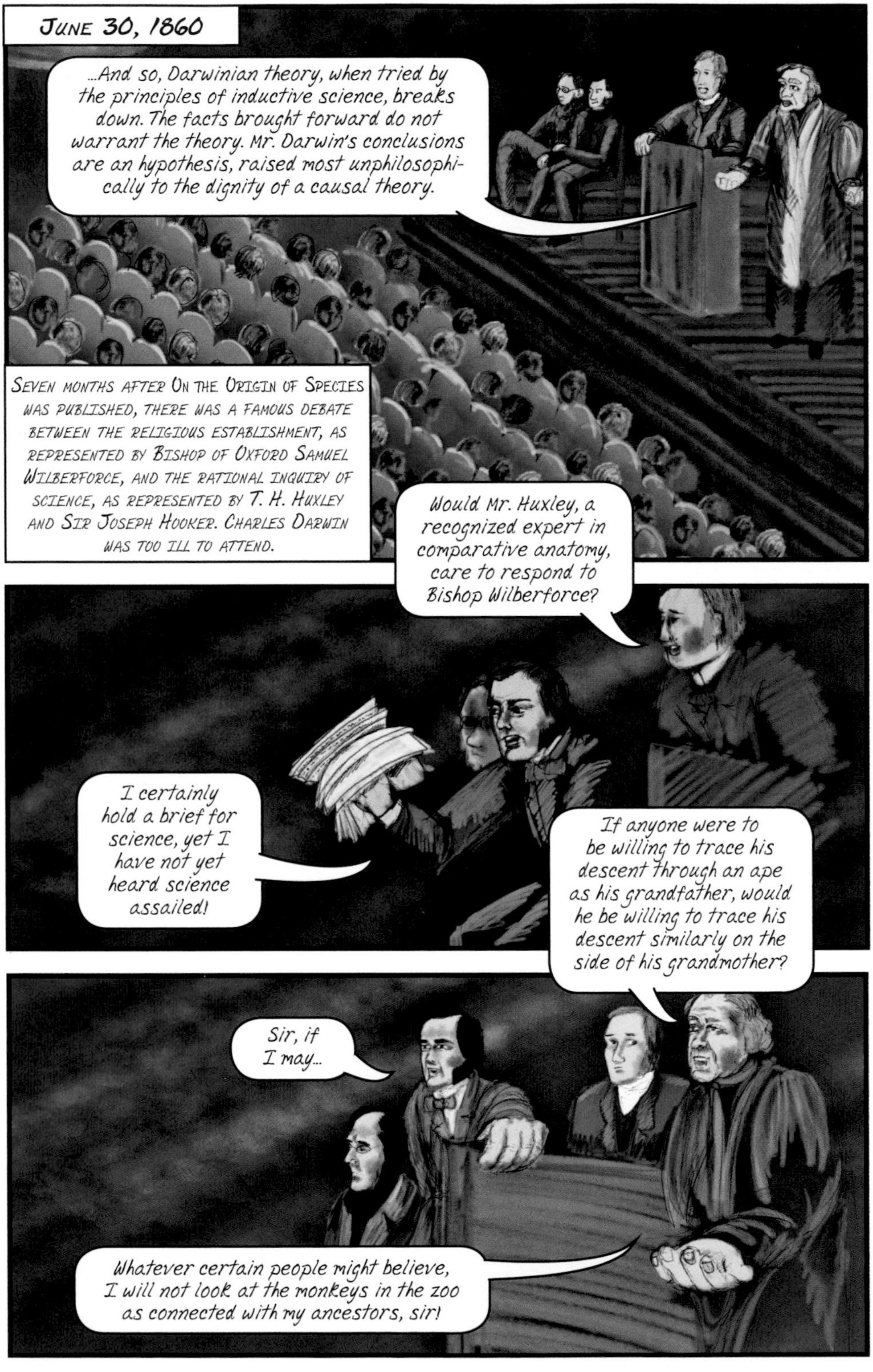

June 30, 1860
...And so, Darwinian theory, when tried by the principles of inductive science, breaks down. The facts brought forward do not warrant the theory. Mr. Darwin's conclusions are an hypothesis, raised most unphilosophically to the dignity of a causal theory.
Seven months after On the Origin of Species was published, there was a famous debate between the religious establishment, as represented by Bishop of Oxford Samuel Wilberforce, and the rational inquiry of science, as represented by T. H. Huxley and Sir Joseph Hooker. Charles Darwin was too ill to attend.
Would Mr. Huxley, a recognized expert in comparative anatomy, care to respond to Bishop Wilberforce?
I certainly hold a brief for science, yet I have not yet heard science assailed!
If anyone were to be willing to trace his descent through an ape as his grandfather, would he be willing to trace his descent similarly on the side of his grandmother?
Sir, if I may...
Whatever certain people might believe, I will not look at the monkeys in the zoo as connected with my ancestors, sir!

Would I rather have a miserable ape for a grandfather or a man highly endowed by nature and possessed of great means of influence and yet who employs those faculties and that influence for the mere purpose of introducing ridicule into a grave scientific discussion? I unhesitatingly affirm my preference for the ape, sir.

With the Origin of Species we now have a structure in which we may make sense of the natural world! It is a framework for finally unlocking the deepest mysteries of life with the power of our intellect!

Oh, myyyy!

Lady Brewster!

I too, sir, affirm my preference for the ape!

And so, my theory, whose roots stretch back to the Greek philosopher Anaximander, leaves my hands and begins its fight for survival among the learned folk and public.

One great hole remains. How is it that individuals inherit the beneficial adaptations of their ancestors?

1865

AUSTRIAN MONK
GREGOR MENDEL

Genius! Why hadn't
I thought of that?!

Ah,
well!

It is quite curious! My work,
with these thousands and thousands of pea plants, seems to be
pointing to some as yet undiscov-
ered general law on the inheritance
of traits from parents to their
offspring.

As scientists would understand later, Mr. Gregor Mendel
had indeed diligently unveiled
a general law of inheritance.
I understood the process of
evolution. He, with his fastidi-
ous experiments, showed us
how to understand that
inheritance is the vehicle that
carries evolution forward.

Our understanding of evolution
has continued to blossom and bear
fruit since then. Many thousands
of scientists from around the
world have contributed along with
a few geniuses, who have pushed
the light of knowledge deeper into
the darkness. I left with so much
more to be done. I must have a
quick look into the future.

A wash of new
evidence will soon begin
coming in, all slowly
erasing objections to
the theory. And, for a
time, other theories
will arise to challenge
natural selection's
primary role in descent
with modification.

174

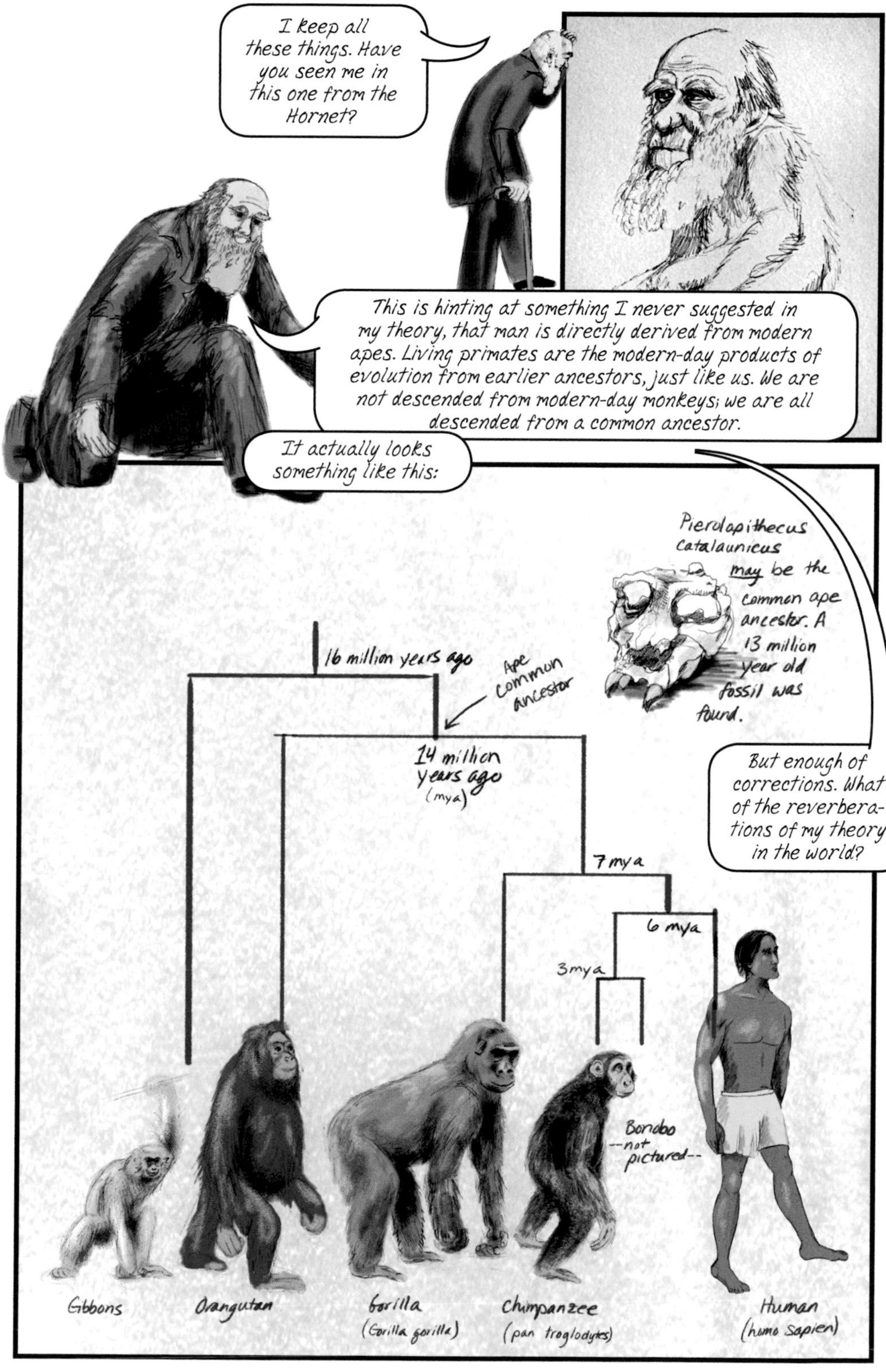

I keep all these things. Have you seen me in this one from the Hornet?
This is hinting at something I never suggested in my theory, that man is directly derived from modern apes. Living primates are the modern-day products of evolution from earlier ancestors, just like us. We are not descended from modern-day monkeys; we are all descended from a common ancestor.
It actually looks something like this:
Pierolapithecus Catalaunicus may be the common ape ancestor. A 13 million year old fossil was found.
16 million years ago
Ape common ancestor
14 million years ago (mya)
7 mya
6 mya
3mya
Bonobo --not pictured--
Gibbons
Orangutan
Gorilla (Gorilla gorilla)
Chimpanzee (pan troglodytes)
Human (homo sapien)
But enough of corrections. What of the reverberations of my theory in the world?

MY LONG ARGUMENT QUICKLY SOLD OUT WHEN IT WAS RELEASED IN NOVEMBER OF 1859 AND WENT THROUGH REPRINTINGS AND NEW EDITIONS. BUT THE IDEA STAYED THE SAME: ALL LIVING THINGS COME FROM ONE OR A FEW ANCIENT COMMON ANCESTORS. AS TIME PASSES, NATURAL SELECTION ACTS TO PICK THE MOST BENEFICIAL VARIATIONS FROM A SPECIES IN EACH GENERATION. THE ACCUMULATION OF BENEFICIAL TRAITS LEADS TO NEW SPECIES.

ON THE ORIGIN OF SPECIES PUBLISHED

1859

1859

WALLACE LINE

ALFRED RUSSEL WALLACE DESCRIBES THE BOUNDARY BETWEEN ASIAN AND AUSTRALIAN ANIMALS, LATER TO BE CALLED THE WALLACE LINE. THIS LINE RUNS THROUGH THE MALAY ARCHIPELAGO, A GROUP OF ISLANDS STRETCHING BETWEEN THE TWO CONTINENTS.

Interesting finding from my dear friend Wallace. This was one of those major observations that launched biogeography, the study of the distribution of the world's life.

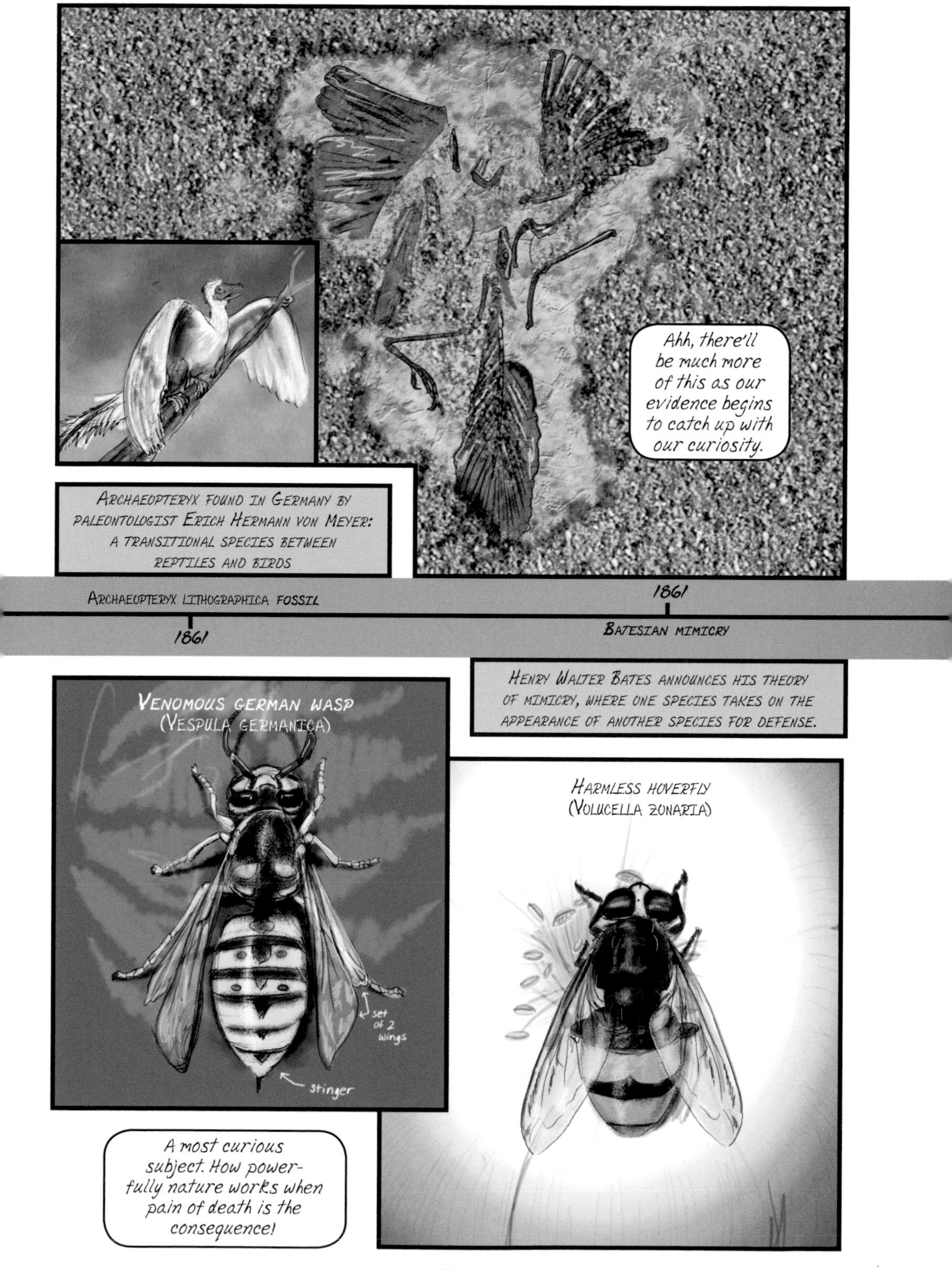
Ahh, there'll be much more of this as our evidence begins to catch up with our curiosity.
ARCHAEOPTERYX FOUND IN GERMANY BY PALEONTOLOGIST ERICH HERMANN VON MEYER: A TRANSITIONAL SPECIES BETWEEN REPTILES AND BIRDS
ARCHAEOPTERYX LITHOGRAPHICA FOSSIL
1861
1861
BATESIAN MIMICRY
HENRY WALTER BATES ANNOUNCES HIS THEORY OF MIMICRY, WHERE ONE SPECIES TAKES ON THE APPEARANCE OF ANOTHER SPECIES FOR DEFENSE.
VENOMOUS GERMAN WASP (VESPULA GERMANICA)
set of 2 wings
stinger
HARMLESS HOVERFLY (VOLUCELLA ZONARIA)
A most curious subject. How powerfully nature works when pain of death is the consequence!

Mmmm, yes. Another piece added to the jigsaw puzzle of man's organic origins among all other living beings. Beautiful.

JAVA MAN (HOMO ERECTUS) DISCOVERED

FIRST HOMINID FOSSIL

1891

1900

MENDELIAN GENETICS

GREGOR MENDEL'S INHERITANCE EXPERIMENTS ON PEA PLANTS ARE REDISCOVERED BY THE WORLD. HE FOUND THAT OFFSPRING DID NOT SHOW THE BLENDED TRAITS OF THEIR TWO PARENTS, BUT INSTEAD PASSED ON DOMINANT AND RECESSIVE ATTRIBUTES AT A STEADY RATIO OF 3 TO 1. HIS STUDIES SHOWED INHERITANCE IS PASSED ON BY AN UNKNOWN SPECIFIC AND DISCRETE ACTOR.

It requires indeed some courage to undertake a labor of such far-reaching extent; this appears, however, to be the only right way by which we can finally reach the solution of a question the importance of which cannot be overestimated in connection with the history of the evolution of organic forms. [Inheritance] follows a constant law, which is founded on the material composition and arrangement of the elements which meet in the cell in a vivifying union.

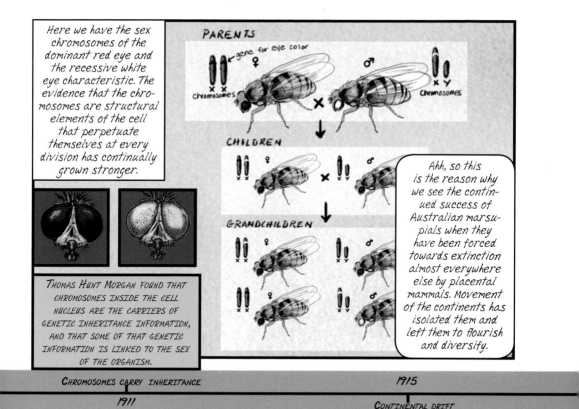

Here we have the sex chromosomes of the dominant red eye and the recessive white eye characteristic. The evidence that the chromosomes are structural elements of the cell that perpetuate themselves at every division has continually grown stronger.

PARENTS

gene for eye color

chromosomes

Chromosomes

CHILDREN

GRANDCHILDREN

Ahh, so this is the reason why we see the continued success of Australian marsupials when they have been forced towards extinction almost everywhere else by placental mammals. Movement of the continents has isolated them and left them to flourish and diversify.

THOMAS HUNT MORGAN FOUND THAT CHROMOSOMES INSIDE THE CELL NUCLEUS ARE THE CARRIERS OF GENETIC INHERITANCE INFORMATION, AND THAT SOME OF THAT GENETIC INFORMATION IS LINKED TO THE SEX OF THE ORGANISM.

CHROMOSOMES CARRY INHERITANCE

1911

1915

CONTINENTAL DRIFT

225 MILLION YEARS AGO

Pangea

200 MILLION YEARS AGO

Laurasia

Gondwanaland

TODAY

ALFRED WEGENER'S THE ORIGINS OF CONTINENTS AND OCEANS DESCRIBES CONTINENTAL DRIFT. ALL THE WORLD'S CONTINENTS USED TO FORM ONE SUPERCONTINENT 225 MILLION YEARS AGO. PLATE TECTONICS CAUSED THE ONE CONTINENT TO SPLIT AND MOVE AROUND THE EARTH. THE SAME FOSSILS ON DIFFERENT CONTINENTS AND THE DISTRIBUTION OF CURRENTLY LIVING ORGANISMS TELL THE STORY THAT ALL LAND WAS JOINED AS ONE.

These were major problems for my theory before we discovered through Mendel's and Fisher's work that dominant and recessive traits are handed down through the generations. Traits do not blend and disappear!

RONALD FISHER BEGINS PIONEERING METHODS TO STATISTICALLY ANALYZE POPULATIONS OF ORGANISMS. HE APPLIED MATHEMATICS TO RECONCILE DARWINIAN NATURAL SELECTION TO MENDELIAN GENETICS. FISHER SHOWS NATURAL SELECTION HAS THE STATISTICAL POWER TO DRIVE ADAPTATION WITHIN THE CONFINES OF THE DISCRETE RATIOS UNDERSTOOD BY GENETICS. ADAPTATION COULD BE SEEN AS A POPULATION'S GENE FREQUENCIES CHANGING OVER TIME. FISHER ALSO SHOWED MENDEL'S LAW OF INHERITANCE MAINTAINS VARIATION IN A POPULATION.

POPULATION BIOLOGY — 1924

1918

POPULATION BIOLOGY

J. B. S. HALDANE BEGINS PUBLISHING PAPERS THAT DESCRIBE QUANTITATIVELY HOW SELECTION CHANGES POPULATIONS OVER TIME.

A satisfactory theory of natural selection must be quantitative!

These three men, Fisher, Haldane and Wright, created the modern study of population genetics, which looks at the evolution of populations through changes in how frequently genes appear. Importantly, their work proved the theoretical foundations of natural selection's compounding effects over time.

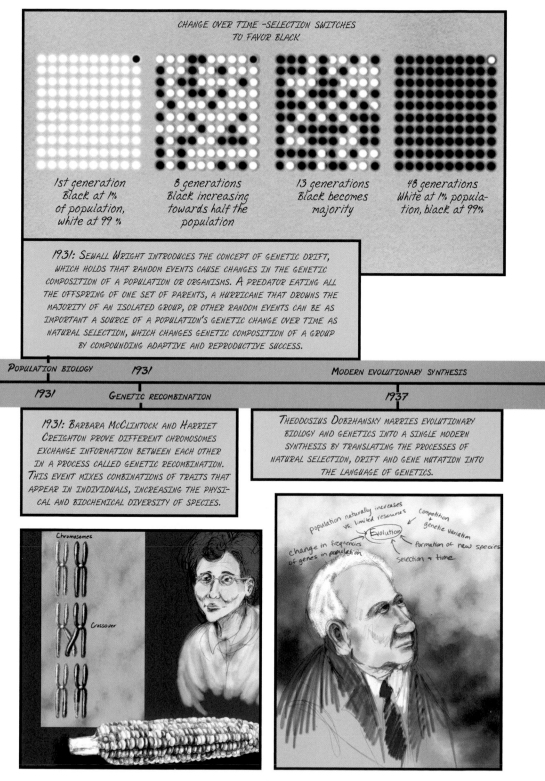

CHANGE OVER TIME —SELECTION SWITCHES
TO FAVOR BLACK

1st generation
Black at 1%
of population,
white at 99 %

8 generations
Black increasing
towards half the
population

13 generations
Black becomes
majority

48 generations
White at 1% popula-
tion, black at 99%

1931: SEWALL WRIGHT INTRODUCES THE CONCEPT OF GENETIC DRIFT,
WHICH HOLDS THAT RANDOM EVENTS CAUSE CHANGES IN THE GENETIC
COMPOSITION OF A POPULATION OR ORGANISMS. A PREDATOR EATING ALL
THE OFFSPRING OF ONE SET OF PARENTS, A HURRICANE THAT DROWNS THE
MAJORITY OF AN ISOLATED GROUP, OR OTHER RANDOM EVENTS CAN BE AS
IMPORTANT A SOURCE OF A POPULATION'S GENETIC CHANGE OVER TIME AS
NATURAL SELECTION, WHICH CHANGES GENETIC COMPOSITION OF A GROUP
BY COMPOUNDING ADAPTIVE AND REPRODUCTIVE SUCCESS.

POPULATION BIOLOGY   1931   MODERN EVOLUTIONARY SYNTHESIS

1931   GENETIC RECOMBINATION   1937

1931: BARBARA MCCLINTOCK AND HARRIET
CREIGHTON PROVE DIFFERENT CHROMOSOMES
EXCHANGE INFORMATION BETWEEN EACH OTHER
IN A PROCESS CALLED GENETIC RECOMBINATION.
THIS EVENT MIXES COMBINATIONS OF TRAITS THAT
APPEAR IN INDIVIDUALS, INCREASING THE PHYSI-
CAL AND BIOCHEMICAL DIVERSITY OF SPECIES.

THEODOSIUS DOBZHANSKY MARRIES EVOLUTIONARY
BIOLOGY AND GENETICS INTO A SINGLE MODERN
SYNTHESIS BY TRANSLATING THE PROCESSES OF
NATURAL SELECTION, DRIFT AND GENE MUTATION INTO
THE LANGUAGE OF GENETICS.

Chromosomes

Crossover

population naturally increases
vs. limited resources

Competition
+
genetic variation

Evolution

change in frequencies
of genes in population

formation of new species

selection + time

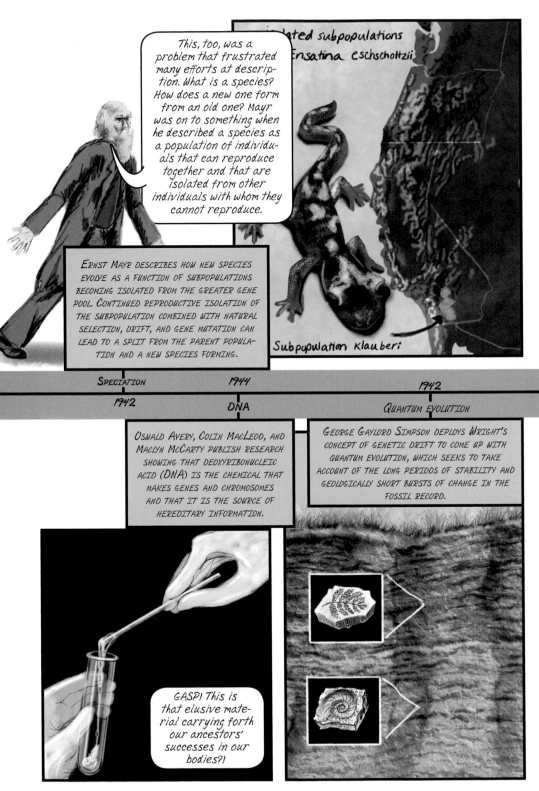

This, too, was a problem that frustrated many efforts at description. What is a species? How does a new one form from an old one? Mayr was on to something when he described a species as a population of individuals that can reproduce together and that are isolated from other individuals with whom they cannot reproduce.

Isolated subpopulations
Ensatina eschscholtzii

ERNST MAYR DESCRIBES HOW NEW SPECIES EVOLVE AS A FUNCTION OF SUBPOPULATIONS BECOMING ISOLATED FROM THE GREATER GENE POOL. CONTINUED REPRODUCTIVE ISOLATION OF THE SUBPOPULATION COMBINED WITH NATURAL SELECTION, DRIFT, AND GENE MUTATION CAN LEAD TO A SPLIT FROM THE PARENT POPULATION AND A NEW SPECIES FORMING.

Subpopulation klauberi

SPECIATION
1942

1944
DNA

1942
QUANTUM EVOLUTION

OSWALD AVERY, COLIN MACLEOD, AND MACLYN MCCARTY PUBLISH RESEARCH SHOWING THAT DEOXYRIBONUCLEIC ACID (DNA) IS THE CHEMICAL THAT MAKES GENES AND CHROMOSOMES AND THAT IT IS THE SOURCE OF HEREDITARY INFORMATION.

GEORGE GAYLORD SIMPSON DEPLOYS WRIGHT'S CONCEPT OF GENETIC DRIFT TO COME UP WITH QUANTUM EVOLUTION, WHICH SEEKS TO TAKE ACCOUNT OF THE LONG PERIODS OF STABILITY AND GEOLOGICALLY SHORT BURSTS OF CHANGE IN THE FOSSIL RECORD.

GASP! This is that elusive material carrying forth our ancestors' successes in our bodies?!

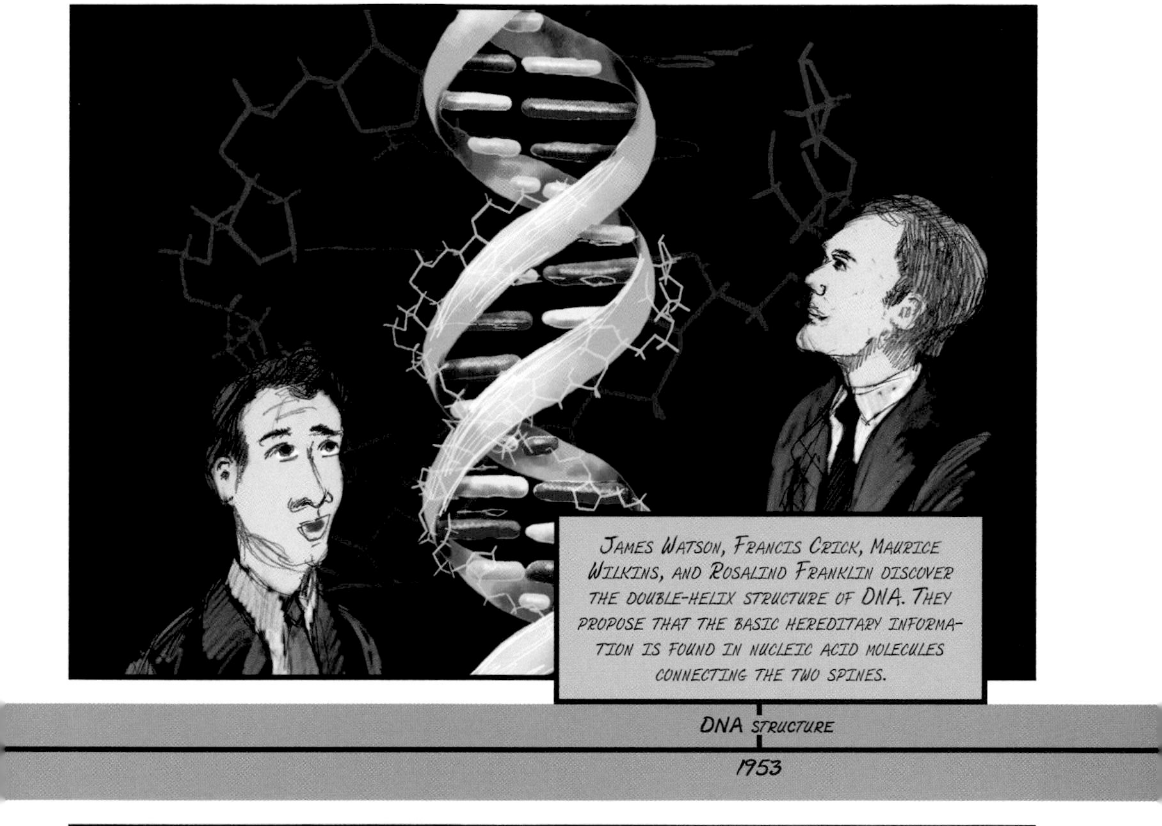
JAMES WATSON, FRANCIS CRICK, MAURICE WILKINS, AND ROSALIND FRANKLIN DISCOVER THE DOUBLE-HELIX STRUCTURE OF DNA. THEY PROPOSE THAT THE BASIC HEREDITARY INFORMATION IS FOUND IN NUCLEIC ACID MOLECULES CONNECTING THE TWO SPINES.

DNA STRUCTURE

1953

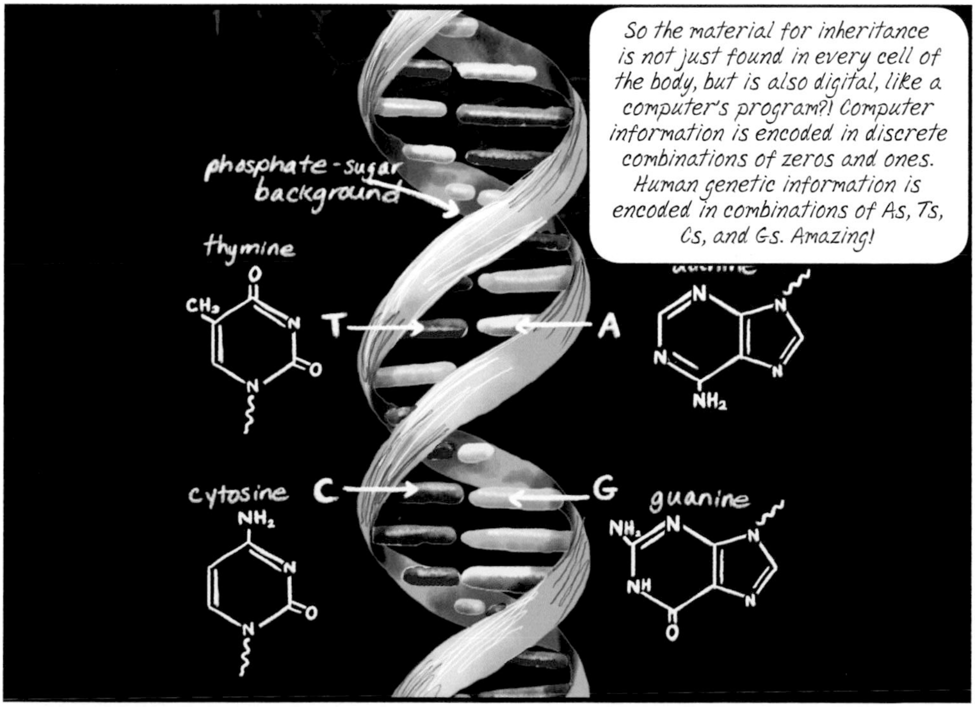
So the material for inheritance is not just found in every cell of the body, but is also digital, like a computer's program?! Computer information is encoded in discrete combinations of zeros and ones. Human genetic information is encoded in combinations of As, Ts, Cs, and Gs. Amazing!
phosphate-sugar background
thymine
T
A
cytosine
C
G
guanine

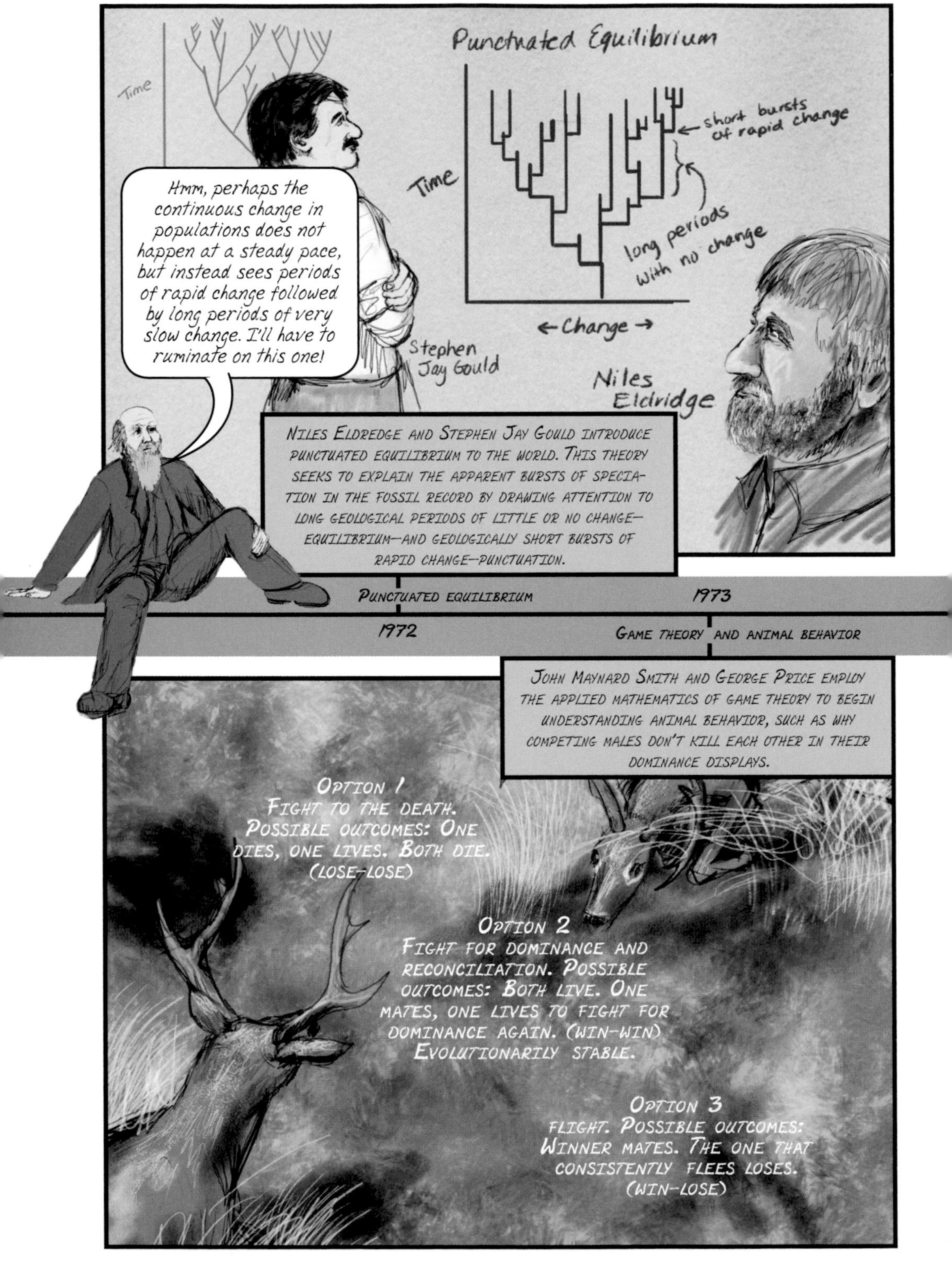
Time
Punctuated Equilibrium
Time
short bursts of rapid change
long periods with no change
← Change →
Stephen Jay Gould
Niles Eldridge
Hmm, perhaps the continuous change in populations does not happen at a steady pace, but instead sees periods of rapid change followed by long periods of very slow change. I'll have to ruminate on this one!
NILES ELDREDGE AND STEPHEN JAY GOULD INTRODUCE PUNCTUATED EQUILIBRIUM TO THE WORLD. THIS THEORY SEEKS TO EXPLAIN THE APPARENT BURSTS OF SPECIATION IN THE FOSSIL RECORD BY DRAWING ATTENTION TO LONG GEOLOGICAL PERIODS OF LITTLE OR NO CHANGE—EQUILIBRIUM—AND GEOLOGICALLY SHORT BURSTS OF RAPID CHANGE—PUNCTUATION.
PUNCTUATED EQUILIBRIUM
1972
1973
GAME THEORY AND ANIMAL BEHAVIOR
JOHN MAYNARD SMITH AND GEORGE PRICE EMPLOY THE APPLIED MATHEMATICS OF GAME THEORY TO BEGIN UNDERSTANDING ANIMAL BEHAVIOR, SUCH AS WHY COMPETING MALES DON'T KILL EACH OTHER IN THEIR DOMINANCE DISPLAYS.
OPTION 1 FIGHT TO THE DEATH. POSSIBLE OUTCOMES: ONE DIES, ONE LIVES. BOTH DIE. (LOSE-LOSE)
OPTION 2 FIGHT FOR DOMINANCE AND RECONCILIATION. POSSIBLE OUTCOMES: BOTH LIVE. ONE MATES, ONE LIVES TO FIGHT FOR DOMINANCE AGAIN. (WIN-WIN) EVOLUTIONARILY STABLE.
OPTION 3 FLIGHT. POSSIBLE OUTCOMES: WINNER MATES. THE ONE THAT CONSISTENTLY FLEES LOSES. (WIN-LOSE)

I too was keenly interested in studying these most important members of the living world. I also reckoned animal behavior was the result of evolutionary processes.

Work like Wilson's helped stoke interest in the phenomenon called emergence, where the simple actions of individuals give rise to complex, organized systems. We can also see emergent organization in the brain's operation and when weather systems develop from disorganized atmospheric conditions. A fascinating field indeed.

E. O. WILSON'S "SOCIOBIOLOGY" SENDS SHOCK WAVES THROUGH SOCIETY BY POSITING THAT ALL ANIMAL BEHAVIOR CAN BEST BE UNDERSTOOD MECHANISTICALLY AS A RESULT OF MOLECULAR BIOLOGY AND EVOLUTION.

SOCIOBIOLOGY

1975

1976

SELFISH GENE

RICHARD DAWKINS POPULARIZES THE CONTROVERSIAL IDEA THAT THE UNIT OF NATURAL SELECTION IS THE GENE, NOT THE ORGANISM OR THE GROUP, AS PREVIOUSLY HELD. THE SELFISH GENE WORKS FOR ITS OWN SURVIVAL AND THE ORGANISM IS ITS VEHICLE.

ATGGTGCATCTGACTCCTGAGGAGAAGT

CTGCCGTTACTGCCCTGTGGGGCAAGGTG

AACGTGGATGAAGTTGGTGGTGAGGCCC

TGGGCAGGTTGGTATCAAGGTTACA...

Section from hemoglobin gene

ALLELE—ONE OF SEVERAL ALTERNATIVE FORMS MAKING UP HOW A GENE IS EXPRESSED IN AN INDIVIDUAL.

hemoglobin allele

hemoglobin allele with sickle cell variant

185

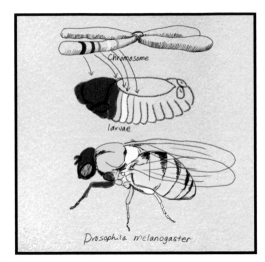

Chromosome

larvae

Drosophila melanogaster

So here we discover there are master switches that when turned on determine the most basic rules of development, such as orientation. I always wondered about that. And here, we begin to understand these very few master switches trigger a cascade of biochemical events leading to development of specific organs and such. The diversity of biological structures is not from an immense number of different instructions, but from these few master switches being turned on and off at different places in the developing organism? Inconceivable.

EDWARD B. LEWIS DETERMINES A SPECIFIC SET OF GENES CONTROL THE MANUFACTURE OF BODY SEGMENTS AND ORGANS IN DEVELOPING EMBRYOS. THOSE GENES ARE LAID OUT ON THE CHROMOSOME IN THE SAME ORDER AS THE BODY SEGMENTS THEY CONTROL. MUTATIONS IN THOSE GENES COULD CAUSE DEFORMITY OR EXTRA SETS OF ORGANS AND SEGMENTS.

Finally, embryology and development come back into the picture to produce some of the most compelling results in evolutionary biology.

GENES AND DEVELOPMENT

1980

1978   GENES AND EMBRYOLOGY

1983

HOMEOBOXES

USING THE FRUIT FLY, CHRISTIANE NÜSSLEIN-VOLHARD AND ERIC F. WIESCHAUS DISCOVER A VERY FEW GENES THAT ARE RESPONSIBLE FOR DETERMINING WHICH END IS THE HEAD, WHICH IS THE TAIL, WHICH WAY IS UP, AND WHICH WAY IS DOWN IN THE EARLIEST STAGES OF EMBRYONIC DEVELOPMENT. THEY ALSO FIND THE GENES CONTROLLING THE NUMBER AND LOCATION OF BODY SEGMENTS.

SCIENTISTS DISCOVER THE EXISTENCE OF HOMEOBOXES, DNA SEGMENTS THAT AMOUNT TO THE MASTER PLAN FOR DEVELOPMENT OF ORGANISMS. RESEARCHERS LATER FIND IDENTICAL HOMEOBOX GENES DISTRIBUTED WIDELY THROUGHOUT THE ANIMAL KINGDOM, FROM INSECTS TO HUMANS.

legs growing in place of antennae

Different types of homeoboxes trigger the development of different structures from the same cells of an organism. One type triggers development of eyes, another causes antennae to develop. The one triggering eye development is found across the animal kingdom, from flies to mice to us. This discovery adds more proof of our descent from a common ancestor.

186

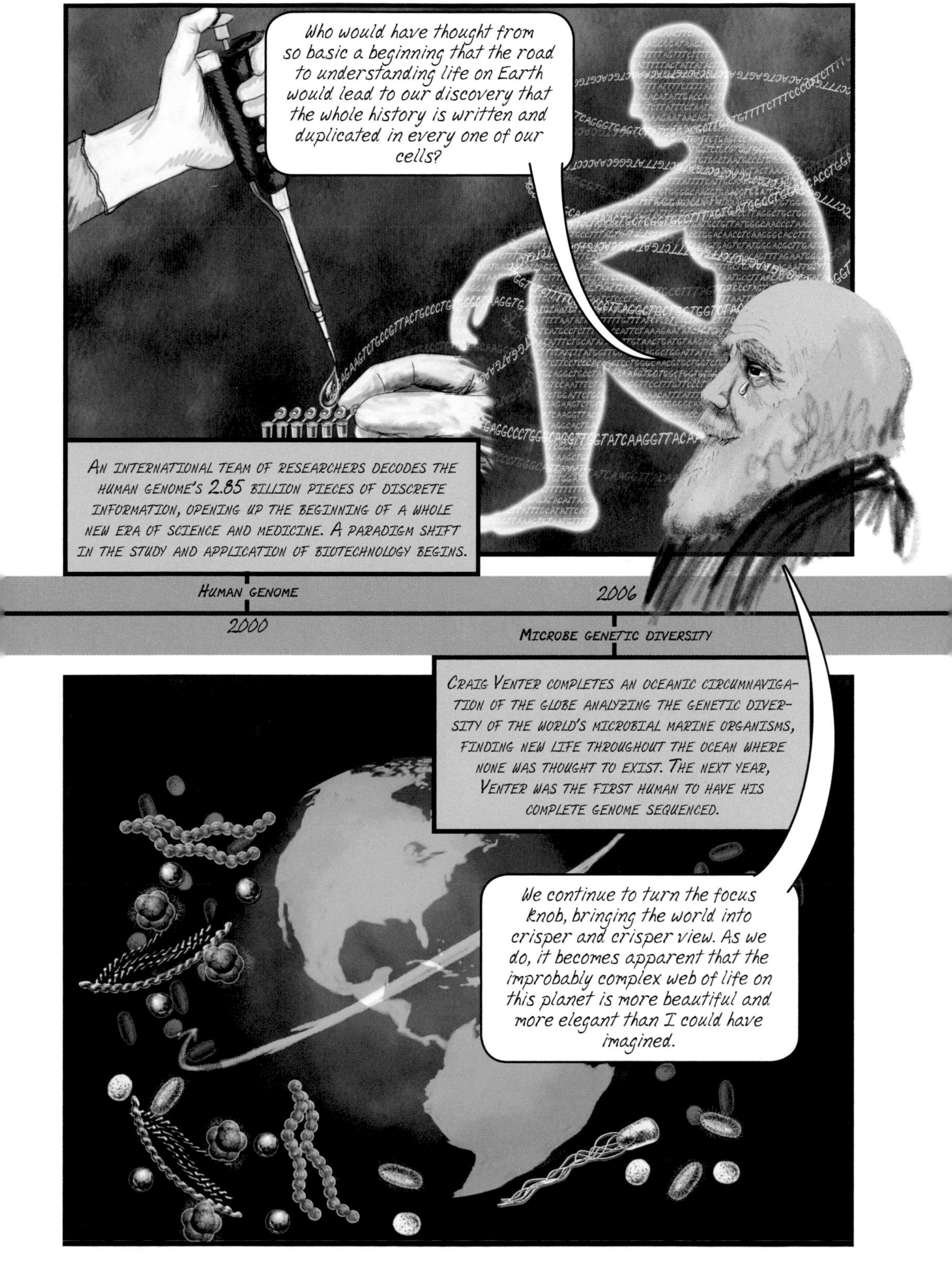
Who would have thought from so basic a beginning that the road to understanding life on Earth would lead to our discovery that the whole history is written and duplicated in every one of our cells?
AN INTERNATIONAL TEAM OF RESEARCHERS DECODES THE HUMAN GENOME'S 2.85 BILLION PIECES OF DISCRETE INFORMATION, OPENING UP THE BEGINNING OF A WHOLE NEW ERA OF SCIENCE AND MEDICINE. A PARADIGM SHIFT IN THE STUDY AND APPLICATION OF BIOTECHNOLOGY BEGINS.
HUMAN GENOME
2000
2006
MICROBE GENETIC DIVERSITY
CRAIG VENTER COMPLETES AN OCEANIC CIRCUMNAVIGATION OF THE GLOBE ANALYZING THE GENETIC DIVERSITY OF THE WORLD'S MICROBIAL MARINE ORGANISMS, FINDING NEW LIFE THROUGHOUT THE OCEAN WHERE NONE WAS THOUGHT TO EXIST. THE NEXT YEAR, VENTER WAS THE FIRST HUMAN TO HAVE HIS COMPLETE GENOME SEQUENCED.
We continue to turn the focus knob, bringing the world into crisper and crisper view. As we do, it becomes apparent that the improbably complex web of life on this planet is more beautiful and more elegant than I could have imagined.

There you have it—our rooted and growing understanding of evolution on Earth. Quite simple, really, when you break it down.

DNA and RNA provide blueprints for cells to create amino acids. Amino acids connect to form proteins. Genetic recombination and mutation randomly inject variability into the genetic information.

The proteins build structures and create biochemical pathways for structures to perform their functions.

Natural selection causes the differential survival of individuals within a species. Helpful or injurious variations affect the chances of individuals to reproduce and carry on those variable genes. Genetic drift and the genes of small founder populations triggered by migration of individuals to new areas also act over time to change species and create new ones.

Natural selection
competition for limited resources

adaptation to change

genetic dr...

migration

structures + functions

genetic recombination + mutation

DNA

RNA

It's beautiful the way it all comes together, isn't it? Like a giant chaotic orchestra, replete with a cast of all the organisms that now exist or have ever existed. There is a grandeur to it.

As individuals adapt to their changing world, they add on more and more changes until they can no longer freely mate with their parent species, and then we may rightly call it a new species—the newest buds on the growing tree of life.

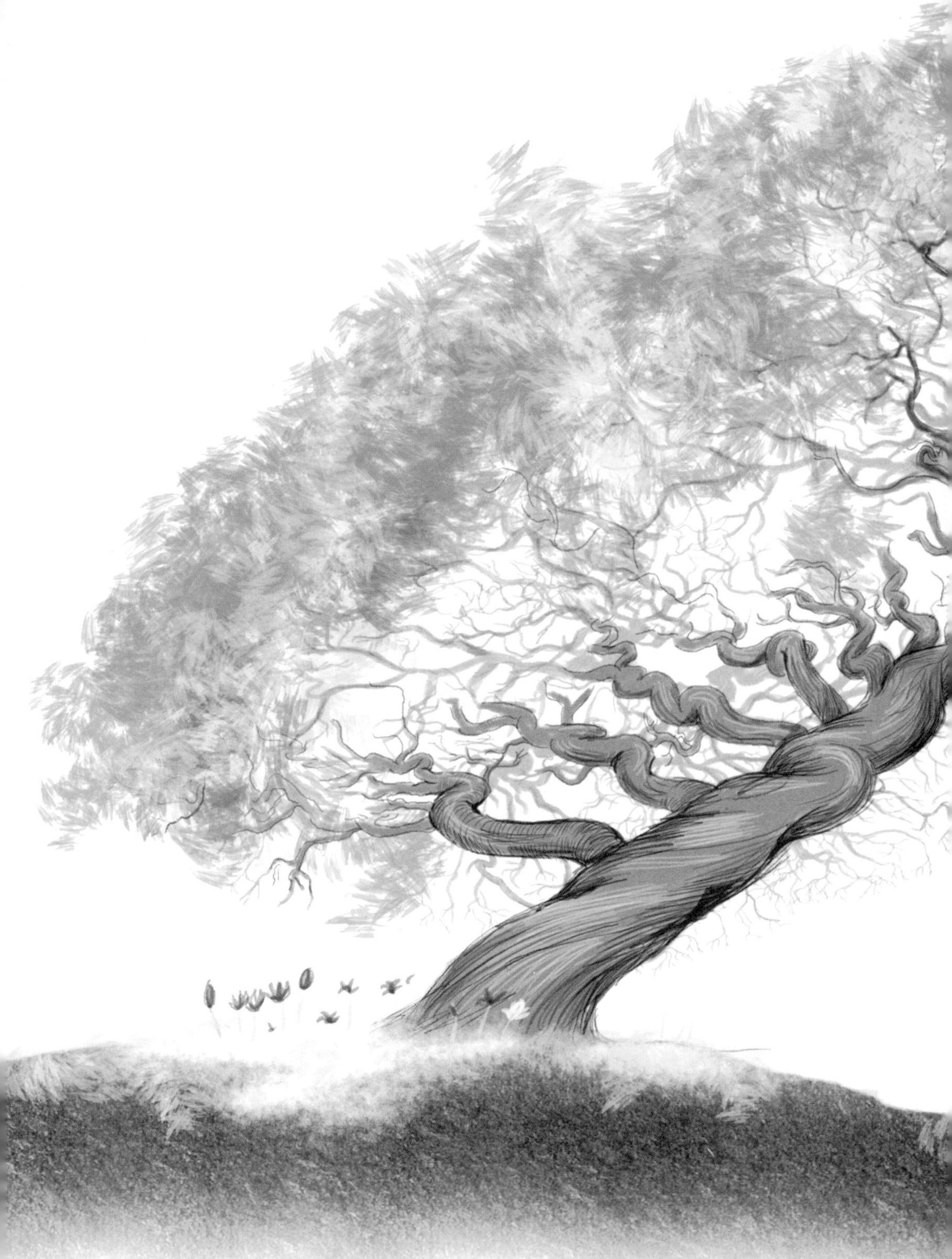

Acknowledgments

Parts of Darwin's correspondence were reproduced in this book. The authors would like to give a heartfelt thanks to Cambridge University and the Darwin Correspondence Project for making the letters publicly available. Darwin's correspondence can be viewed online at www.darwinproject.ac.uk or in the published Correspondence of Charles Darwin, Cambridge University Press.

The authors wish to thank Janet Browne, a great scholar who helped us get to know Darwin, and the scientists who dedicate their lives to uncovering the beauty of nature's machinery. Finally, the authors wish to give their hearty thanks to their agents Frank and Richard at Venture Literary, who conceived the possibility of this work.

Michael Keller dedicates this book to the friends and family who have given him shelter, comfort, friendship, guidance, and assistance over the years. He specifically thanks Mom and Dad, Zola and Ave Keller, for their unwavering support and unconditional love in even the most trying times. He is lucky to have them both. Thanks, too, to Genese and Bill Fine, friends who asked for nothing but a gumbo recipe after they gave him their home during the writing of this book.

Nicolle Rager Fuller thanks the family and friends who have believed in her over the years, and more recently, put up with her long absence while being immersed in work. In particular she'd like to thank her husband Jason for his patience, love, keen eye, and good cooking; and her mom, dad, and brothers Matthew and Adam for their unwavering support and the example set by their lifelong enthusiasm for learning.